Gardening
Month by Month
in Ontario

Alison Beck

Lone Pine Publishing

© 2003 by Lone Pine Publishing
First printed in 2003   10 9 8 7 6 5 4 3 2
Printed in Canada

The Publisher: Lone Pine Publishing
10145 – 81 Avenue
Edmonton, AB, Canada T6E 1W9
Website: www.lonepinepublishing.com

1808 B Street NW, Suite 140
Auburn, WA, USA 98001

National Library of Canada Cataloguing in Publication Data
Beck, Alison, 1971-
  Gardening month by month in Ontario / Alison Beck.

  ISBN 1-55105-361-6

  1. Gardening--Ontario. I. Title.
SB453.3.C2B445 2002   635'.09713   C2002-911433-0

Editorial Director: Nancy Foulds
Project Editor: Sandra Bit
Researchers: Don Williamson, Laura Peters, Carol Woo
Production Coordinator: Jennifer Fafard
Design & Layout: Heather Markham
Cover Design: Gerry Dotto
Production Support: Elliot Engley, Jeff Fedorkiw, Lana Anderson-Hale, Lynett McKell
Principal Photographers: Tamara Eder, Tim Matheson, Robert Ritchie
Illustrations: Ian Sheldon
Scanning, Separations & Film: Elite Lithographers Co.

Front cover photographs (left to right) by Tamara Eder, golden marguerite, forsythia, poppy, painted tongue, sweet potato vine; *by Tim Matheson*, daylily, dahlia, calendula

The photographs in this book are reproduced with the generous permission of their copyright holders.

Additional photos: All-American Selections 99c, 127b, 129a; Therese D'Monte 70; Don Doucette 23b; Elliot Engley 31a, 31c, 33a, 33b; EuroAmerican 19a; Jennifer Fafard 123c, 125b, 125c, 127a, 129c, 131a, 131b, 132–133, 137b, 151a, 151b, 151c, 155b, 155c; Anne Gordon 137c; Saxon Holt 144–45, 148; Horticolor© Nova-Photographik/Horticolor 94; Linda Kershaw 39b, 39c; Colin Laroque 96–97; Dawn Loewen 36–37; Erika Markham 117b; Heather Markham 57b, 75a, 81c; Kim O'Leary 29b, 143b; Allison Penko 27b, 113c; Laura Peters 81b, 81d, 115a, 119c; Peter Thomstone 45b, 51c, 105a, 141a; Don Williamson 119a, 135a.

Frost date maps: information taken from *The Atlas of Canada* (http://atlas.gc.ca) ©2002. Her Majesty the Queen in Right of Canada with permission of Natural Resources Canada. *Climate normals and extremes charts*: adapted from the Meteorological Service of Canada, with permission from Environment Canada.

We acknowledge the financial support of the Government of Canada through the Book Publishing Industry Development Program (BPIDP) for our publishing activities.

PC: 08

ƟNTRODUCTION

One of my first gardening memories is of hauling all the frost-heaved stones out of the vegetable beds of our garden near the Ottawa River. It seemed that no matter how many buckets or wheelbarrows full of rocks we added every year to the long stone pile that ran along the back of the property, there were always more the next year. The vegetables grew fabulously and tasted great, but it's the rocks I really remember.

Gardening in Ontario is wonderful. It has so much to offer gardeners. The summers are warm and long, and the winters are cold enough to keep plants dormant and encourage good blooming in the spring. The soil, though not without its challenges, supports a variety of healthy plants. The geological diversity also influences how gardeners garden. The Canadian Shield dominates the north and east of Ontario. Here rock gardens and rock walls are always in style, often by necessity. The soil may consist of clay or sand and is often quite acidic. In contrast, gardeners living near the limestone-rich Niagara Escarpment, which skirts the southern tip of Lake Ontario and heads north to the Bruce Peninsula, work with alkaline soils. Fertile river valleys and ancient floodplains dominate in the south, but may also be found here and there all over the province.

The natural ecoregions of Ontario are widely diverse, ranging from tundra and boreal forest in the north to mixed forest in the south. Seeing what grows naturally in an area can indicate what will grow well in our gardens. The variety of plant material and designs displayed in Ontario gardens is a true indication of the broad selection gardeners here have to choose from.

violas

Because Ontario is a huge, complex province, gardeners in Thunder Bay may feel as if they have nothing in common with gardeners in Niagara Falls. A stroll through a garden in each city would probably show how wrong this idea is. Many of the same plants will grow in gardens all over Ontario.

Though many books still reflect the presumed hardiness of certain plants, Ontario gardening catalogues and garden centres are beginning to give gardeners a more accurate picture of what will grow here. Many plants that were previously declared simply 'out of zone' are now referred to as 'hardy in many Ontario gardens.' Every imaginable style of garden can be and probably has been created here, from free-form English-style cottage gardens to cool, moist woodland gardens and from Zen-like Japanese gardens to formal knot gardens. These gardens reflect the style and enthusiasm of the gardeners and the diversity of situations in which they garden.

Where we garden varies almost as much as what we garden. Apartment and condo dwellers enjoy container gardening; rural gardeners may be tilling the same

an Ontario garden

soil that many generations of their ancestors did; urban gardens include those in older neighbourhoods with deep topsoil and those whose brand new gardens may have only the thin layer of soil the construction company returned to their yards. Beautiful, successful gardens are possible in every situation, limited only by the imagination of the gardener.

The climate is not without its challenges, and some research and experimentation are required to get the best results from your garden. The short growing season in the north, lack of snowcover in the south, damage caused by ice storms, summer humidity and too much or too little rain are all climatic challenges gardeners in Ontario face. The key to cold-climate gardening is not how cold it

gazanias

bridge pathway (*above*); mini alpine garden (*below*)

naturalistic water feature (*below*)

gets, but keeping everything consistently cold. Generally, cycles of freezing and thawing, wet soil and dehydrating winds do more damage than the cold itself. Learning what to expect and when to expect it as well as what plants are best suited to your garden are key elements to gardening anywhere, not just in Ontario.

During the growing season, adequate precipitation can make the difference between gardening success or failure. In a good year, regular rainfall takes care of all our watering needs and only hanging baskets and beds beneath the overhang of the house need to be watered. In a bad year, it seems as if it will never stop raining or that it will never rain again. Although rainfall is fairly dependable, droughts and deluges are always possible. As with all the factors that influence our gardens, we must be prepared to make the most of what nature offers us and try to take up the slack where it lets off.

The length of the growing season also varies greatly. Some northern gardeners have only 90 frost-free days to work with, while some of their southern counterparts enjoy 180 days between the last and first frost dates. Northern gardens will have more hours of sunlight during the summer months, which makes up somewhat for the shorter growing season.

Many of the gardening books available to us are written by and for gardeners who have never done much cold-climate gardening. Most of the general information about gardening is accurate and useful, but hardiness information, for example, is often based on assumption and guesswork and not always on experimentation and knowledge. It is almost always worth trying a plant, even if it isn't supposed to be hardy. It may very well thrive in a sheltered spot in your garden or with an insulating layer of snow.

The purpose of this book is to give you ideas and to help you plan what should be done and when. Garden tasks are listed in the month they should be completed, and

mixed border

general ideas that can be applied in a variety of months are also included. There is plenty of space for you to write in your own thoughts and ideas.

The information in this book is general. If you need more detailed information on a topic, refer to the resource listed at the back of the book. Your local library is also an excellent place to search for the information you need. Gardening courses are offered through colleges, continuing education programs, gardening societies and through Master Gardener programs. You can tackle even the most daunting garden task once you are prepared and well informed.

golden marguerite

delphinium with rudbeckia (black-eyed Susan)

Use this book to keep track of unusual weather conditions, when plants sprout and when they first flower. Make note of the birds and insects you see in the garden. If a plant gave you a lot of trouble in a certain location, you will remember not to put it in the same location next year if you add that comment to your book. Jot down your fantastic inspirations for future gardening design plans. If you see an unfamiliar and exciting plant at a garden centre or in a neighbourhood garden, you can make a note to look it up later. Write down anything about your garden that tickles your fancy. You'll appreciate it next spring when memories of this year's garden are getting a little fuzzy.

There are no absolute rules when it comes to gardening. No two years are identical, and all information should be taken with a pinch of salt. Use your own best judgement when deciding when to do things in your garden. If spring has been cold and wet you may have to plant later than suggested, or earlier if an early spring warms things up quickly.

Above all else, always take time to enjoy your Ontario garden.

hot peppers

ONTARIO CLIMATE NORMALS 1971–2000

(Adapted from the Meteorological Service of Canada data
as posted on the Environment Canada website)

	CATEGORY	JAN	FEB	MAR	APR	MAY	JUN	JUL	AUG	SEP	OCT	NOV	DEC	YEAR
BARRIE	DAILY MAXIMUM (°C)	-3.2	-2.0	3.2	10.6	18.1	23.4	26.0	24.8	20.1	13.2	6.1	0.0	11.7
	DAILY MINIMUM (°C)	-12.8	-12.1	-7.5	0.0	6.5	12.0	15.0	14.2	9.6	3.7	-1.4	-7.9	1.6
	RAINFALL (MM)	15.3	13.3	28.9	57.8	77.2	86.6	73.4	92.6	97.6	74.3	62.1	21.3	700.2
	SNOWFALL (CM)	80.2	39.5	28.1	5.0	0.1	0.0	0.0	0.0	0.0	2.5	20.6	62.4	238.4
	PRECIPITATION (MM)*	95.4	52.8	57.0	62.9	77.3	86.6	73.4	92.6	97.6	76.8	82.6	83.7	938.5
KENORA	DAILY MAXIMUM (°C)	-12.6	-7.9	-0.5	9.0	17.4	21.8	24.4	23.1	16.4	8.9	-1.5	-9.9	7.4
	DAILY MINIMUM (°C)	-22.0	-17.8	-10.6	-1.8	6.2	11.6	14.5	13.3	7.4	1.3	-8.2	-18.3	-2.0
	RAINFALL (MM)	0.4	2.7	6.9	19.8	63.0	107.7	95.3	85.8	80.2	42.7	9.3	0.6	514.4
	SNOWFALL (CM)	28.0	17.9	22.3	13.6	1.5	0.1	0.0	0.0	0.8	11.4	35.2	27.4	158.2
	PRECIPITATION (MM)	26.1	19.3	27.7	32.7	64.3	107.8	95.3	85.8	81.2	53.7	42.3	25.7	661.8
KINGSTON	DAILY MAXIMUM (°C)	-3.2	-2.6	2.8	10.0	16.5	21.4	24.8	24.0	19.5	13.0	6.8	0.4	11.1
	DAILY MINIMUM (°C)	-12.2	-11.7	-5.9	0.8	7.1	12.1	15.7	15.0	10.4	4.4	-0.7	-8.1	2.2
	RAINFALL (MM)	31.5	28.1	47.5	74.8	74.9	72.3	58.8	88.1	93.0	86.4	84.9	54.3	794.6
	SNOWFALL (CM)	46.1	37.0	29.9	9.2	0.3	0.0	0.0	0.0	0.0	1.1	9.8	47.6	180.9
	PRECIPITATION (MM)	73.5	62.1	79.5	84.9	75.2	72.3	58.8	88.1	93.0	87.5	94.5	99.0	968.2
LONDON	DAILY MAXIMUM (°C)	-2.4	-1.4	4.2	11.6	19.0	23.8	26.3	25.2	20.9	14.0	6.9	0.6	12.4
	DAILY MINIMUM (°C)	-10.1	-9.7	-4.7	1.0	7.0	12.1	14.6	13.7	9.6	4.0	-0.7	-6.5	2.5
	RAINFALL (MM)	31.1	29.1	53.8	73.8	82.6	86.8	82.2	85.3	97.7	74.9	73.7	47.0	817.9
	SNOWFALL (CM)	52.6	38.1	28.6	9.2	0.3	0.0	0.0	0.0	0.0	2.7	19.7	51.1	202.4
	PRECIPITATION (MM)	74.2	60.0	78.4	82.2	82.9	86.8	82.2	85.3	97.7	77.6	91.1	88.6	987.1
NIAGARA FALLS	DAILY MAXIMUM (°C)	-1.0	-0.5	5.1	12.2	19.3	24.2	27.2	26.0	21.3	14.7	8.0	1.9	13.2
	DAILY MINIMUM (°C)	-7.9	-7.7	-3.2	2.4	8.6	13.9	17.2	16.7	12.5	6.4	1.3	-4.7	4.6
	RAINFALL (MM)	27.2	28.5	55.6	68.2	75.6	87.5	75.4	81.6	95.2	83.7	79.4	50.6	808.6
	SNOWFALL (CM)	42.4	38.9	20.0	7.3	0.9	0.0	0.0	0.0	0.0	0.6	11.6	40.1	161.6
	PRECIPITATION (MM)	69.5	67.4	75.5	75.5	76.5	87.5	75.4	81.6	95.2	84.3	91.0	90.7	970.2
OTTAWA	DAILY MAXIMUM (°C)	-6.1	-3.9	2.1	10.9	19.1	23.8	26.4	25.0	19.7	12.6	4.9	-2.9	11.0
	DAILY MINIMUM (°C)	-14.8	-13.2	-7.0	1.1	8.0	13.0	15.5	14.3	9.7	3.7	-1.9	-10.3	1.5
	RAINFALL (MM)	22.9	16.1	33.6	59.7	80.9	91.2	88.9	87.6	86.8	76.2	60.5	28.8	733.2
	SNOWFALL (CM)	48.7	41.2	32.1	7.5	0.2	0.0	0.0	0.0	0.0	3.0	18.0	52.2	202.7
	PRECIPITATION (MM)	64.2	51.6	64.9	67.7	81.0	91.2	88.9	87.6	86.8	79.1	77.0	74.1	914.2

*equivalent to rainfall

ONTARIO CLIMATE NORMALS 1971–2000
(Adapted from the Meteorological Service of Canada data
as posted on the Environment Canada website)

OWEN SOUND

CATEGORY	JAN	FEB	MAR	APR	MAY	JUN	JUL	AUG	SEP	OCT	NOV	DEC	YEAR
DAILY MAXIMUM (°C)	-2.2	-1.7	3.0	9.8	16.6	21.4	24.5	23.8	19.6	13.3	6.5	0.7	11.3
DAILY MINIMUM (°C)	-9.4	-9.5	-5.4	0.8	6.1	11.1	14.9	14.8	11.0	5.7	0.5	-5.4	2.9
RAINFALL (MM)	23.8	19.9	39.8	61.6	71.8	76.3	72.6	88.6	105.2	86.5	73.9	32.9	752.8
SNOWFALL (CM)	110.9	58.1	37.6	8.7	0.2	0.0	0.0	0.0	0.0	2.3	35.5	93.9	347.2
PRECIPITATION (MM)	134.8	78.0	77.4	70.2	72.0	76.3	72.6	88.6	105.2	88.8	109.4	126.9	1100.1

SAULT STE. MARIE

CATEGORY	JAN	FEB	MAR	APR	MAY	JUN	JUL	AUG	SEP	OCT	NOV	DEC	YEAR
DAILY MAXIMUM (°C)	-5.5	-4.2	0.9	8.4	16.5	21.1	24.0	23.0	18.0	11.5	4.1	-2.2	9.6
DAILY MINIMUM (°C)	-15.5	-15.2	-9.7	-2.2	3.5	7.9	11.3	11.3	7.5	2.5	-3.1	-10.3	-1.0
RAINFALL (MM)	7.8	4.7	28.0	50.5	62.5	78.4	76.8	84.7	96.2	80.3	50.7	13.7	634.3
SNOWFALL (CM)	81.7	42.8	34.8	17.4	0.5	0.0	0.0	0.0	0.2	6.2	38.6	80.8	302.9
PRECIPITATION (MM)	71.3	41.1	60.1	68.5	63.1	78.4	76.8	84.7	96.5	86.7	85.7	75.9	888.7

SUDBURY

CATEGORY	JAN	FEB	MAR	APR	MAY	JUN	JUL	AUG	SEP	OCT	NOV	DEC	YEAR
DAILY MAXIMUM (°C)	-8.4	-6.1	-0.1	8.5	17.2	22.0	24.8	23.1	17.3	10.0	2.0	-5.1	8.8
DAILY MINIMUM (°C)	-18.6	-16.6	-10.4	-2.2	5.3	10.4	13.3	12.3	7.2	1.5	-5.1	-13.9	-1.4
RAINFALL (MM)	12.5	7.1	29.8	47.0	75.9	77.7	76.6	90.7	101.2	76.8	47.6	13.7	656.5
SNOWFALL (CM)	63.8	50.0	38.9	18.3	1.5	0.0	0.0	0.0	0.1	5.3	32.4	64.2	274.4
PRECIPITATION (MM)	68.6	50.6	65.9	64.9	77.5	77.8	76.6	90.5	101.3	82.1	76.5	67.1	899.3

THUNDER BAY

CATEGORY	JAN	FEB	MAR	APR	MAY	JUN	JUL	AUG	SEP	OCT	NOV	DEC	YEAR
DAILY MAXIMUM (°C)	-8.6	-5.6	0.3	9.0	16.4	20.6	24.2	23.1	17.1	10.4	1.7	-6.1	8.5
DAILY MINIMUM (°C)	-21.1	-18.4	-11.2	-3.3	2.5	7.3	11.0	10.1	4.9	-0.5	-7.7	-17.0	-3.6
RAINFALL (MM)	2.5	2.8	17.5	29.5	65.0	85.7	89.0	87.5	87.5	57.0	31.5	3.6	559.0
SNOWFALL (CM)	41.2	26.9	26.8	12.4	1.7	0.0	0.0	0.0	0.5	6.1	27.8	44.1	187.6
PRECIPITATION (MM)	31.3	24.9	41.6	41.5	66.5	85.7	89.0	87.5	88.0	62.6	55.6	37.5	711.6

TORONTO

CATEGORY	JAN	FEB	MAR	APR	MAY	JUN	JUL	AUG	SEP	OCT	NOV	DEC	YEAR
DAILY MAXIMUM (°C)	-1.1	-0.2	4.6	11.3	18.5	23.5	26.4	25.3	20.7	13.8	7.4	1.8	12.7
DAILY MINIMUM (°C)	-7.3	-6.3	-2.0	3.8	9.9	14.8	17.9	17.3	13.2	7.3	2.2	-3.7	5.6
RAINFALL (MM)	29.1	26.2	42.0	63.2	73.3	71.5	67.5	79.6	83.4	64.7	67.3	41.9	709.8
SNOWFALL (CM)	38.2	26.6	22.0	6.0	0.0	0.0	0.0	0.0	0.0	0.1	8.1	32.2	133.1
PRECIPITATION (MM)	61.2	50.5	66.1	69.6	73.3	71.5	67.5	79.6	83.4	64.7	75.7	71.0	834.0

WINDSOR

CATEGORY	JAN	FEB	MAR	APR	MAY	JUN	JUL	AUG	SEP	OCT	NOV	DEC	YEAR
DAILY MAXIMUM (°C)	-0.9	0.6	6.4	13.4	20.5	25.4	27.9	26.6	22.5	15.6	8.3	1.9	14.0
DAILY MINIMUM (°C)	-8.1	-7.0	-2.4	3.0	9.3	14.7	17.4	16.6	12.3	6.2	0.9	-4.8	4.9
RAINFALL (MM)	28.7	33.3	55.6	80.7	80.7	89.8	81.8	79.7	96.2	64.1	67.3	47.3	805.2
SNOWFALL (CM)	35.0	27.5	20.6	4.3	0.0	0.0	0.0	0.0	0.0	0.7	8.3	30.1	126.6
PRECIPITATION (MM)	57.6	57.3	75.0	85.1	80.8	89.8	81.8	79.7	96.2	64.9	75.5	74.7	918.3

ONTARIO CLIMATE EXTREMES 1971–2000

(Adapted from the Meteorological Service of Canada data
as posted on the Environment Canada website)

BARRIE

MAXIMUM (°C)	36.0 ON JULY 6, 1988
MINIMUM (°C)	-35.0 ON JANUARY 4, 1981
DAILY RAINFALL (MM)	96.0 ON JUNE 2, 1995
DAILY SNOWFALL (CM)	65.0 ON JANUARY 9, 1978
SNOW DEPTH (CM)	59.0 ON FEBRUARY 9, 2001

KENORA

MAXIMUM (°C)	35.8 ON JULY 14, 1983
MINIMUM (°C)	-43.9 ON JANUARY 20, 1943
DAILY RAINFALL (MM)	153.5 ON JULY 27, 1993
DAILY SNOWFALL (CM)	36.3 ON APRIL 10, 1957
SNOW DEPTH (CM)	145.0 ON MARCH 5, 1966

KINGSTON

MAXIMUM (°C)	34.3 ON JULY 15, 1983
MINIMUM (°C)	-34.5 ON JANUARY 4, 1981
DAILY RAINFALL (MM)	128.8 ON SEPTEMBER 14, 1979
DAILY SNOWFALL (CM)	46.2 ON DECEMBER 16, 1974
SNOW DEPTH (CM)	64.0 ON DECEMBER 22, 1977

LONDON

MAXIMUM (°C)	38.2 ON JUNE 25, 1988
MINIMUM (°C)	-31.7 ON JANUARY 24, 1970
DAILY RAINFALL (MM)	89.1 ON SEPTEMBER 29, 1986
DAILY SNOWFALL (CM)	57.0 ON DECEMBER 7, 1977
SNOW DEPTH (CM)	70.0 ON DECEMBER 10, 1977

NIAGARA FALLS

MAXIMUM (°C)	38.3 ON AUGUST 26, 1948
MINIMUM (°C)	-25.0 ON FEBRUARY 15, 1943
DAILY RAINFALL (MM)	95.3 ON AUGUST 24, 1954
DAILY SNOWFALL (CM)	45.7 ON FEBRUARY 19, 1940
SNOW DEPTH (CM)	47.0 ON MARCH 3, 1984

OTTAWA

MAXIMUM (°C)	37.8 ON JULY 4, 1913
MINIMUM (°C)	-38.9 ON DECEMBER 29, 1933
DAILY RAINFALL (MM)	93.2 ON SEPTEMBER 9, 1942
DAILY SNOWFALL (CM)	55.9 ON JANUARY 29, 1894
SNOW DEPTH (CM)	97.0 ON FEBRUARY 24, 1971

OWEN SOUND

MAXIMUM (°C)	35.0 ON JUNE 10, 2000
MINIMUM (°C)	-34.0 ON FEBRUARY 18, 197
DAILY RAINFALL (MM)	75.7 ON AUGUST 19, 1968
DAILY SNOWFALL (CM)	62.0 ON DECEMBER 10, 199!
SNOW DEPTH (CM)	88.0 ON DECEMBER 12, 199!

SAULT STE. MARIE

MAXIMUM (°C)	36.8 ON JULY 7, 1988
MINIMUM (°C)	-38.9 ON JANUARY 23, 1948
DAILY RAINFALL (MM)	116.6 ON MAY 31, 1970
DAILY SNOWFALL (CM)	61.0 ON FEBRUARY 10, 1947
SNOW DEPTH (CM)	140.0 ON DECEMBER 12, 199

SUDBURY

MAXIMUM (°C)	38.3 ON JULY 31, 1975
MINIMUM (°C)	-39.3 ON JANUARY 10, 1982
DAILY RAINFALL (MM)	112.0 ON SEPTEMBER 3, 197
DAILY SNOWFALL (CM)	38.8 ON MARCH 10, 1992
SNOW DEPTH (CM)	145.0 ON MARCH 16, 1959

THUNDER BAY

MAXIMUM (°C)	40.3 ON AUGUST 7, 1983
MINIMUM (°C)	-41.1 ON JANUARY 30, 1951
DAILY RAINFALL (MM)	131.2 ON SEPTEMBER 8, 197
DAILY SNOWFALL (CM)	51.6 ON JANUARY 20, 1956
SNOW DEPTH (CM)	179.0 ON JANUARY 22, 1956

TORONTO

MAXIMUM (°C)	40.6 ON JULY 8, 1936
MINIMUM (°C)	-32.8 ON JANUARY 10, 1859
DAILY RAINFALL (MM)	98.6 ON JULY 27, 1897
DAILY SNOWFALL (CM)	48.3 ON DECEMBER 11, 194
SNOW DEPTH (CM)	65.0 ON JANUARY 15, 1999

WINDSOR

MAXIMUM (°C)	40.2 ON JUNE 25, 1988
MINIMUM (°C)	-29.1 ON JANUARY 19, 1994
DAILY RAINFALL (MM)	94.6 ON APRIL 20, 2000
DAILY SNOWFALL (CM)	36.8 ON FEBRUARY 25, 1965
SNOW DEPTH (CM)	42.0 ON FEBRUARY 9, 1982

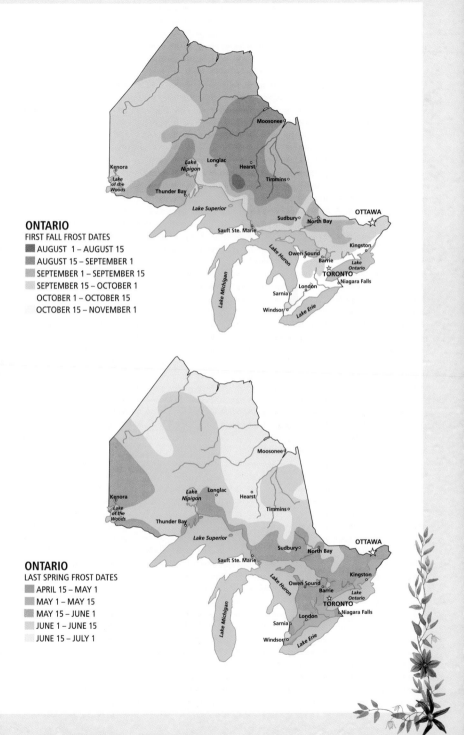

ONTARIO
FIRST FALL FROST DATES
- AUGUST 1 – AUGUST 15
- AUGUST 15 – SEPTEMBER 1
- SEPTEMBER 1 – SEPTEMBER 15
- SEPTEMBER 15 – OCTOBER 1
- OCTOBER 1 – OCTOBER 15
- OCTOBER 15 – NOVEMBER 1

ONTARIO
LAST SPRING FROST DATES
- APRIL 15 – MAY 1
- MAY 1 – MAY 15
- MAY 15 – JUNE 1
- JUNE 1 – JUNE 15
- JUNE 15 – JULY 1

JANUARY

Now is the time for planning and
dreaming of the distant summer
and the garden yet to be.

JANUARY

1

2

Avoid using chemical de-icers because they are harmful to lawns and garden plants.

3

4

If you had a real Christmas tree, instead of recycling, cut it up and use the branches as a mulch to shelter low-growing shrubs and groundcovers.

5

6

7

One of the flowers you might dream of adding to your garden in spring is the beautiful hybrid tea 'Loving Memory' (*left*). This zone 5 rose will flourish in most Ontario gardens in a sheltered spot.

Cotoneaster (*right*)

In most years, the garden is blanketed in snow by January, but southern Ontario gardens are just as likely to be bare and exposed to the fluctuations in temperature. South-facing walls are always warmer than other areas of the garden. Snow melts most quickly here, leaving plants vulnerable to the stressful cycles of heat and cold. A good, thick fall mulch proves to be extremely valuable in a snowless year or a snowless area.

THINGS TO DO

January is one of the hardest months for the garden and the easiest for the gardener.

Water shrubs and evergreens during winter thaws if there is no snow around them. Water the ground around the plants, but don't worry if some water freezes onto the branches—the ice won't hurt them.

Don't forget to top up your bird-feeders regularly. Feeding the birds encourages them to keep visiting in summer when they will help keep your insect pest populations under control.

Snow is the garden's best friend. Pile clean snow on snowless garden beds to insulate them against the wind and cold. Some people refer to this as "snow farming."

8

9

Avoid placing houseplants in hot or cold drafts.

10

11

Order gardening and seed catalogues to look through even if you don't start your own seeds.

12

13

14

Begonias (*left*) can be brought indoors in fall and kept as houseplants in a sunny location through the winter.

Gently brush snow off the branches of evergreens such as cedars, but leave any ice that forms to melt naturally. The weight of the snow or ice can permanently bend flexible branches, but more damage is done trying to remove ice than is done through its weight.

Choose and order seeds for early starting. Sort through the seeds you have, test them for viability and throw out any that don't germinate or that you won't grow. Trade seeds with gardening friends.

Get lawn mowers and other power tools serviced now. They will be ready for use in spring, and you may get a better price before the spring rush.

Annual poppy seeds are easy to collect and share with friends. There are many colour choices available in both single- (*Iceland poppies, centre right*) and double-flowering (*peony-flowered poppies, top right and below*) varieties.

To test older seeds for viability, place 10 seeds between two layers of moist paper towel and put them in a sealed container. Keep the paper evenly dampened but not too wet. Seeds may rot if the paper towel is too moist. Check each day to see if the seeds have sprouted. If less than half the seeds sprout, buy new ones.

15

16

Reduce watering of houseplants because most need little water during winter.

17

18

19

20

The datura is an elegant, exotic-looking plant that produces large, showy, scented flowers. Daturas should be brought indoors in winter.

Coleus (*top right*); English ivy topiary (*bottom right*)

Clean the foliage of your house-plants. When light levels are low, it is important for plants to be able to use whatever light is available. As a bonus, you might help reduce insect populations because their eggs will likely be wiped off along with the dust.

Check houseplants regularly for common indoor insect pests such as whiteflies, spider mites and mealybugs.

GARDEN DESIGN

As you look out your windows at the frozen yard, think about what could make your garden look attractive in winter. Features such as birdbaths, ponds, benches, decks and winding pathways improve the look and function of your garden year-round. Persistent fruit, unusual bark and branch patterns, evergreens and colourfully stemmed shrubs also provide winter interest.

Most indoor plants will benefit from increased humidity levels. Place pots on a tray of pebbles. If you add water to the pebbles when needed, you will increase the humidity through evaporation but prevent water-logged roots.

JANUARY

21

22

January is a great time for garden planning.
In winter, the bones of the garden are
laid bare, so you can take a good look
at the garden's overall structure.

23

24

25

26

27

Rosehips (*left*), the coppery bark of amur cherry
and the bright berries of viburnum (*top right*),
the seedpods of amur maple (*centre right*), and
the curving branches of Japanese maple (*bottom
right*) add interest to the garden in winter.

Plants that add variety to a winter garden:

- Shrub Roses (*Rosa*): brightly colored hips
- Dogwoods (*Cornus*): red, purple or yellow stems
- Maples (*Acer ginnala*, *Acer palmatum*): attractive bark and branching patterns
- Winged Euonymus (*Euonymus alatus*): corky ridges on the branches
- Highbush Cranberry (*Viburnum trilobum*): bright red berries
- Cedar (*Thuja*), False Cypress (*Chamaecyparis*) or Juniper (*Juniperus*): evergreen branches
- Corkscrew Hazel (*Corylus*): twisted and contorted branches
- Clematis (*Clematis*): fuzzy seedheads
- Cotoneaster (*Cotoneaster*): persistent red berries
- Kerria (*Kerria*): bright green stems
- Amur Cherry (*Prunus maackii*): coppery, peeling bark

28	29

*Imagine the garden you'd like to have,
and keep a notebook and your diagrams
at hand so you can jot down ideas
as they come to you.*

30	31

Woody evergreens,
such as cedar (*left*),
upright juniper (*top
right*) and white spruce
(*far right*), add
interesting texture and
rich green colour to a
sometimes monotonous
winter landscape.

PROBLEM AREAS IN THE GARDEN

Keep track of these potential problem areas in your garden.

- windswept areas: perhaps a tree, shrub or hedge could be added next summer to provide shelter

- snowfree areas: places where the snow is always quick to melt are poor choices for very tender plants, which benefit most from the protection of the snow

- snowbound areas: places where the snow is slowest to melt provide the most protection to plants but stay frozen longest in spring, making them poor locations for spring-flowering plants

Spruce are widely grown in Ontario, and new varieties are available almost every gardening season. They are well suited to our winters, and some, such as the Colorado blue spruce (*left*), provide wonderful winter colour against brilliant white snow.

FEBRUARY

The longer days and occasional warm spells turn our thoughts to the upcoming gardening season.

FEBRUARY

1

2

Finish ordering plants and seeds from catalogues.

3

4

During warm spells, water plants not covered by snow.

5

6

7

Colourful little crabapples often remain on the branches of the tree through winter, a reminder of the beautiful blossoms to come in spring (*left and top right*).
Flowering crabapple trees in spring (*bottom right*)

Groundhog Day is a teaser for Ontario gardeners. By February we all want winter to be over soon, but more often than not, the cold and snow stay around. Gardening can get under way, however. February is a great month for starting seeds and keeping a close eye on the garden during those warm, potentially dry spells.

THINGS TO DO

February is another month with few tasks, but preparations can be made now that will keep things moving smoothly once the season kicks into high gear.

Check shrubs and trees for storm-damaged branches, and remove them using proper pruning techniques.

Cut branches of flowering shrubs, such as forsythia, crabapple and cherry, to bring indoors. Placed in a bright location in a vase of water, they will begin to flower, giving you a taste of spring in winter.

FEBRUARY

8

9

*Continue to check for insect pests on
your houseplants.*

10

11

*Thoroughly clean empty planters,
containers and seed trays to get them
ready for spring planting.*

12

13

14

Dianthus (*left*), browallia (*top right*),
bellflower (*far right*) and begonia (*near right*)
are plants you can start from seed in February.

Start seeds for annuals, perennials and vegetables that are slow to mature. A few to consider are

- Geranium (*Pelargonium*)
- Amethyst Flower (*Browallia*)
- Bellflower (*Campanula*)
- Begonia (*Begonia*)
- Hollyhock (*Alcea*)
- Lady's Mantle (*Alchemilla*)
- Pinks (*Dianthus*)
- Tomatoes (*Lycopersicon*)
- Peppers (*Capsicum*)

Starting plants from seed is a great way to propagate a large number of plants at a relatively low cost. You can grow plants you can't find at any garden centre and get a jump-start on the growing season.

FEBRUARY

15

16

Keep seedlings in the brightest location available to reduce stretching.

17

18

Check to see if any of the tubers or bulbs you are storing indoors have started sprouting. Pot them and keep them in a bright location once they do.

19

20

21

Many varieties of dahlia (*left*) can be started from seed in February for transplanting after the danger of frost has passed.

Fresh herbs growing in a greenhouse in winter (*centre right*); seed tray, pots, soil and spray mister for indoor seeding (*bottom right*)

As the days start to lengthen, indoor plants may start to show signs of new growth. Increase watering and apply a weak fertilizer (1/4 strength) only after they begin to grow.

Seedlings will be weak and floppy if they don't get enough light. Consider purchasing a fluorescent or other grow light (*above*) to provide extra illumination for them.

STARTING SEEDS

There are a few things you will need for starting seeds:

- containers to grow them in, such as pots, trays or peat pots
- sterile soil mix intended for starting seeds
- plastic bags or tray covers to keep the seedbed humid.

Tips for growing healthy seedlings:

- Transplant seedlings to individual containers once they have three or four true leaves to prevent crowding.
- Space plants so that the leaves do not overshadow those of neighbouring plants.

FEBRUARY

22

23

*After seeds have been planted,
and once seedlings emerge, moisten the
soil with a hand-held spray mister when
the soil begins to dry out.*

24

25

*Don't fertilize young seedlings. Wait until
the seed leaves (the first leaves to appear)
have begun to shrivel, then fertilize with a
weak fertilizer once a week.*

26

27

28

29

The floribunda rose 'Fellowship/Livin' Easy' (*left*)
is well known for its reliable vigour, attractive foliage
and showy, long-lived blooms. It also makes a great
cut flower.

Tips for starting seeds:

- Moisten the soil before you fill the containers.
- Firm the soil down in the containers, but don't pack it too tightly.
- Leave seeds that require light for germination uncovered.
- Plant large seeds individually by poking a hole in the soil with the tip of a pen or pencil and then dropping the seed in the hole.
- Spread small seeds evenly across the soil surface, then lightly cover with more soil mix.
- To spread small seeds, place them in the crease of a folded piece of paper and gently tap the bottom of the fold to roll them onto the soil (*top right*).
- Mix very tiny seeds, like those of begonia, with very fine sand before planting to spread them out more evenly.
- Plant only one type of seed in each container. Some seeds will germinate before others, and it is difficult to keep both seeds and seedlings happy in the same container.
- Cover pots or trays of seeds with clear plastic to keep them moist (*right*).
- Seeds do not need bright, direct light to germinate and can be kept in an out-of-the-way place until they begin to sprout.
- Once the seeds germinate, keep the seedlings in a bright location and remove the plastic cover.

A hand-held spray mister and a heating coil or pad are useful, but not required.

To prevent seedlings from damping-off, always use a sterile soil mix, thoroughly clean containers before using them, maintain good air circulation around seedlings and water from the bottom, keeping the soil moist, not soggy.

FEBRUARY

Envision the garden you want rather than the garden you have by designing your own garden layout (*below*). Garden design can be as simple as planting a container to display on your patio or deck, or it can be more complex, involving a variety of beds and borders or the addition of features such as shelters and walkways (*opposite page*).

N

FLOWERBED

FLOWERING
CRABAPPLE

PATIO

HOUSE

FLOWERBED

FLOWERBED

WALKWAY

RED
MAPLE

DRIVEWAY

GARDEN PLANNING

Using graph paper, plot out the existing yard and house:

- Put in trees, shrubs and other solid structural elements. If you remember where the flowerbeds are, add those as well. Garden beds can be added later if you're not sure. Make copies and use them to keep track of your plans.

- Create a master plan and then sub-plans so you can keep track of the changes you'd like to make each year.

- Make another plan of just your vegetable garden, if you have one, so you can plan and keep track of crop rotations.

MARCH

*Expect the unexpected in March. Our gardens
can be under a blanket of snow one day
and showing the first signs of spring the next.*

MARCH

1

2

Prune off any growth on your trees and shrubs that was damaged over winter.

3

4

The single most important thing you can do when planting is to make sure you have the right plant in the right location. Consider the mature size of the plant and its cultural requirements.

5

6

When designing your garden, consider planting a fast-growing, drought-tolerant elder (*left and near right*). The elder's showy foliage adds colour and texture to a landscape, and its edible berries can be made into jelly or wine or left for the birds.

Prune dogwoods (*top right and far right*) after flowering.

7

Early warm spells lure us out to see what's sprouting. Witch-hazel unfolds its spidery flowers, hellebores open from beneath the melting snow and the earliest spring bulbs herald in the much anticipated spring. Just when we think winter is over, a late snowfall blankets the garden and we go back to planning.

THINGS TO DO

The first few tasks of spring get us out in the garden by late March.

Days can be warm enough to encourage some plants to start sprouting. Keep snow piled on beds or mulches topped up to protect plants from the freezing nights.

MARCH

8

9

As the snow melts, start clearing up the debris in your yard, such as leaves, sticks, garbage and doggie poop.

10

11

Prune late-flowering shrubs (July or later) and shrubs grown for colourful young growth.

12

13

14

As soon as the snow begins to melt in spring, the leaves of the bergenia become visible and are quickly followed by its pretty magenta flowers (*left*).

Spirea (*top right*); hardy kiwi (*centre right*); hydrangea (*bottom right*)

Keep off your lawn when it is frozen, bare of snow and/or very wet to avoid damaging the grass or compacting the soil.

Apply horticultural oil (also called dormant oil), used to control over-wintering insects, to trees, shrubs and vines before the buds swell. Follow the directions carefully to avoid harming beneficial insects.

Plants to prune in spring
- Red-twig Dogwood (*Cornus alba*)
- Yellow or Purple-leafed Elders (*Sambucus*)
- Hydrangea (*Hydrangea*)
- Hardy Kiwi (*Actinidia arguta*)
- Potentilla (*Potentilla*)
- Japanese Spirea (*Spirea japonica*)
- False Spirea (*Sorbaria sorbifolia*)

MARCH

15

16

Start indoor seeding. Most of the seeds you may wish to start early can be started by late March.

17

18

Water houseplants that start sprouting new growth more frequently, and apply a weak fertilizer.

19

20

21

Bigleaf hydrangea (*left*) is a popular shrub but needs a very protected site and moist soil to survive in Ontario gardens.

If planted early enough in spring, clematis (*top right*) flowers the first summer.

PLANTING IN SPRING

As March draws to a close, we head into prime planting season. Trees, shrubs, vines and perennials often establish most quickly when they are planted just as they are about to break dormancy. They are full of growth hormones, and they recover quickly from transplant shock.

Avoid using dormant oil on blue-needled evergreens, such as blue spruce (*above and below*). The treatment takes the blue off the existing needles, though the new needles will be blue.

MARCH

22

23

Before doing any digging, call your utility companies to locate any buried wires, cables or pipes to prevent injury and save time and money.

24

25

Don't plant vigorous spreaders in rock gardens with tiny alpine plants or large shrubs right next to walkways.

26

27

28

In Ontario, rhododendrons (*left*) grow well and look good when planted in groups. They thrive in sheltered locations and require fertile, acidic, moist and well-drained soil to do well.

Flowering quince (*top right*); goat's beard (*bottom right*)

A few things to keep in mind when planting your garden:

- Never work with your soil when it is very wet or very dry.

- Avoid planting during the hottest, sunniest part of the day. Choose an overcast day, or plant early or late in the day.

- Prepare your soil before you plant to avoid damaging roots later.

- Get your new plants into the ground as soon as possible when you get them home. Roots can get hot and dry out quickly in containers. Keep plants in a shady spot if you must wait to plant them.

- Most plants are happiest when planted at the same depth they have always grown at. Trees, in particular, can be killed by too deep a planting.

- Remove containers before planting. Plastic and fibre pots restrict root growth and prevent plants from becoming established.

- Plants should be well watered when they are newly planted. Watering deeply and infrequently will encourage the strongest root growth.

- Check the root zone before watering. The soil surface may appear dry when the roots are still moist.

MARCH

29

30

*If a plant needs well-drained soil
and full sun to thrive, it will be healthiest
and best able to fight off problems in
those conditions. Work with your plants'
natural tendencies.*

31

The splendid yellow shrub rose 'Morden Sunrise'
(*below*) is one of the few yellow roses hardy
enough for any Ontario garden.

Harden annuals and perennials off before planting them by gradually exposing them to longer periods of time outside. Doing so gives your plants time to adapt to outdoor weather conditions and reduces the chance of transplant shock.

Remove only damaged branches when planting trees or shrubs, and leave the plant to settle in for at least one year before you begin any formative pruning. Plants need all the branches and leaves they have when they are trying to get established.

Trees less than 1.5 m (5') tall do not need staking unless they are in a very windy location. Unstaked trees develop stronger root systems.

staking a tree properly

planting a balled-and-burlapped tree

planting a bare-root tree

APRIL

The snow melts, the garden comes to life,
sprouting and flowering.
We know that spring is finally here.

APRIL

1

2

Plant trees, shrubs and vines once the soil can be worked.

3

4

Check your power tools, such as the lawn mower, and have them serviced if you didn't do it over winter.

5

6

7

The columbine (*left*) is a beautiful flower that some say resembles a bird in flight. Its jewel-like colours herald the coming of summer.

Clockwise from top right: primroses; foxgloves; lungwort

Take a trip to a garden centre. The best selection of uncommon annuals and perennials is available early, and you may be able to purchase woody plants while they are still dormant. Many garden centres will take your name and call you when the plants you are looking for arrive.

The warm days of spring are welcome, but we know that cold frosty nights and perhaps a late spring flurry are also likely. The first green shoots emerge, and we are eager to get out in the garden. April frosts are almost inevitable in most of Ontario, but by the end of the month we feel assured that warm days and summer are just around the corner. We finish our tidying and watch as our gardens awaken.

APRIL

8

9

Pull back mulch from sprouting plants on warm days, but be prepared to cover plants back over on cold nights.

10

11

Clean up the garden. Rake debris off lawns and prune back old perennial growth.

12

13

14

Consider planting daylilies (*left*) this spring. Though each bloom lasts only a day, these lilies are easy going, prolific and versatile, and come in an almost infinite variety of forms, sizes and colours.

Magnolia (*top right*); California poppies (*bottom right*)

THINGS TO DO

The real gardening work begins—raking, digging, planting and pruning. We begin the hard work that will let us sit back and enjoy the garden once summer arrives.

Bring garden tools out of storage and examine them for rust or other damage. Clean and sharpen them if you didn't before you put them away in fall.

Store any plants you have purchased or started indoors in as bright a location as possible. You may begin to harden them off by placing them outdoors for a short period each day.

Avoid working your soil until it has thawed and dried out a bit. A handful of thawed soil should squeeze into a ball that holds its shape but breaks easily apart when pressed with a thumb or finger.

Seeds sown directly into the garden may take longer to germinate than those planted indoors, but the resulting plants, such as poppies (*below*), will be stronger.

15

16

Divide perennials that bloom in mid-summer or later, such as asters, daylilies and sedums.

17

18

Cool, wet spring weather can cause some drought-loving plants to rot. Improve soil drainage through the addition of organic matter.

19

20

21

A traditional garden favourite, sweet peas (*left*) are easy to grow from seed in spring. They sprout quickly and have sweetly scented blooms that can be cut often for fragrant indoor bouquets.

Clockwise from top right: phlox, cabbage, rocket larkspur and nigella be planted before the last spring frost.

Warming up vegetable beds with row covers allows many plants and seeds to be sown early.

Many plants prefer to grow in cool weather and can be started well before the last frost. These seeds can be planted as soon as the soil can be worked:

- Spinach (*Spinacea oleracea*)
- Peas (*Pisum sativum*)
- Swiss Chard (*Beta vulgaris*)
- Cabbage (*Brassica oleracea*)
- Kale (*Brassica napus*)
- Bachelor's Buttons (*Centaurea cyanus*)
- Calendula (*Calendula officinalis*)
- California Poppy (*Eschscholzia californica*)
- Godetia (*Clarkia amoena*)
- Love-in-a-Mist (*Nigella damascena*)
- Phlox (*Phlox drummondii*)
- Poppy (*Papaver rhoeas*)
- Rocket Larkspur (*Consolida ajacis*)
- Sweet Pea (*Lathyrus odoratus*)

APRIL

22

23

Repot houseplants if needed.

24

25

*Tomatoes, snapdragons and spiderflowers
can be started from seed only a few weeks
before moving them into the garden.*

26

27

28

You can depend on aubretia (*left*) to put on
a great floral show in spring.

Clockwise from top right: spiral
juniper; pompom cedar;
formally pruned yew hedge
and cedars

PRUNING

Prune trees and shrubs to maintain the health and attractive shape of a plant, increase the quality and yield of fruit, control and direct growth and create interesting plant forms and shapes.

Once you learn how to prune plants correctly, it is an enjoyable garden task. There are many good books available on the topic of pruning. One is listed at the back of this book. If you are unsure about pruning, take a pruning course, often offered by garden centres, botanical gardens and adult education programs.

Don't prune trees or shrubs when growth has started and buds are swelling. Prune before growth starts in spring or wait until plants have leafed out.

Clockwise from top right: climbing rose with support; espalier; proper secateur orientation

PRUNING TIPS

- Prune at the right time of year. Trees and shrubs that flower before June, usually on the previous year's wood, should be pruned after they have flowered. Trees and shrubs that flower after June, usually on new growth, can be pruned in spring.

- Use the correct tool for the size of branch to be removed: secateurs, or hand pruners, for growth up to 2 cm (3/4") in diameter; long-handled loppers for growth up to 4 cm (1 1/2") in diameter; or a pruning saw for growth up to about 15 cm (6") in diameter.

- Always use clean and sharp tools.

- Always use secateurs or loppers with the blade side towards the plant and the hook towards the part to be removed.

thinning cuts

Thin trees and shrubs to promote the growth of younger, healthier branches. Doing so rejuvenates a plant.

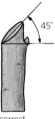

45°

correct

too low

angle too great

too high

When pruning, avoid the following:

- Don't leave stubs. Whether you are cutting off a large branch or deadheading a lilac, always cut back to a join. Branches should be removed to the branch collar, and smaller growth should be cut back to a bud or branch union. There is no absolute set angle for pruning. Each plant should be pruned according to its individual needs.

- Never use pruning paint or paste. Trees have a natural ability to create a barrier between living and dead wood. Painting over a cut impairs this ability.

- Never try to remove a tree or large branch by yourself. Have someone help you, or hire a professional to do it.

Always hire an ISA (International Society of Arboriculture) certified professional to remove branches on trees growing near power lines or other hazardous areas, especially if they could damage a building, fence or car if they were to fall. Branches and trees are usually much heavier than anticipated and can do a lot of damage if they fall in the wrong place.

MAY

The promise of spring is fulfilled with
the sprouting and blooming of May,
and winter is soon forgotten.

MAY

1

2

Move or divide any perennials that didn't have enough space last summer.

3

4

Prune early flowering shrubs, such as forsythia, once they are finished flowering, if needed.

5

6

7

The Japanese anemone or windflower (*left*) is an attractive plant at all stages. Some varieties bloom in spring while others reserve their lovely display for fall.

Saucer magnolia (*top right*) flowers in mid– to late spring; the combination of tulips and pansies (*bottom right*) makes an interesting colour and height contrast in a spring flowerbed.

May weather can still be unpredictable, one year warm and sunny and the next cold and wet. In a typical May, bulbs are blooming, peonies poke up their red and green spears and spring-flowering trees like magnolia and crabapple burst forth in a riot of colour. Even the most devoted lawn-lover knows that spring is truly here when the first dandelion of spring, tucked up against a south wall, opens its fuzzy face to the sun.

THINGS TO DO

A new gardening season awaits, one where we haven't forgotten to weed or water, where all our plants are properly spaced and well staked and where no insects have chewed any leaves. Now is the time to finish tidying up the garden, prepare the garden beds and get the planting done.

MAY

8

9

Begin to harden off any houseplants you plan to move outdoors for summer.

10

11

Work compost into your garden beds and fork them over, removing weeds as you go, to prepare them for planting later in the month.

12

13

14

Clematis such as C. 'Gravetye Beauty' (*left*) is a popular perennial vine with beautiful, showy flowers in many shapes and sizes. By planting a variety of them, you can have clematis in bloom from spring to fall.

Clockwise from top right: C. 'Hagley Hybrid'; C. integrifolia; C. viticella 'Etoile Violette'

Remove mulch from perennials and trim back and clear away any of last year's growth if it was still too cold to do so in April.

Clear away any of the annuals or vegetables that didn't make it to the compost pile last fall.

By the end of the month, you will have a good idea of what has been damaged or killed back over winter, and you can trim or remove plants as needed.

Accept that grass will not grow everywhere. Grass requires plenty of sun and regular moisture. Many trees and buildings provide too much shade and don't allow enough water to penetrate the soil for grass to grow successfully. Use mulch or other groundcovers in areas where you have trouble growing grass. When selecting trees to plant in the lawn, choose ones that will provide only light shade and that will enjoy the plentiful water they will be sharing with the grass, or have a grass-free zone extending from the base of the tree to the dripline.

15

16

Continue to harden off your early-started seedlings and purchased plants so they will be ready to plant outside when the weather is warm enough.

17

18

When planning your vegetable garden, consider planting extra to donate to a local food bank or homeless shelter. Even if you just end up with the inevitable extra zucchini and tomatoes, they can be put to good use.

19

20

21

Plant a sunny spring flower such as doronicum (*left*) with tulips and forget-me-nots to create a cheerful May display.

It is possible to have a healthy, attractive organic lawn. Grass is an extremely competitive plant, capable of fighting off invasions by weeds, pests and diseases without the use of chemicals. Watering with compost tea encourages a healthy lawn.

Lawns need very little water to remain green. Watering deeply and infrequently will encourage deep roots that are not easily damaged during periods of drought. Five millimetres (1/4") of water a week will keep grass alive and 2.5 cm (1") a week will keep it green (*below*).

The official last frost date falls between April 15 and May 24, depending on the year and where in Ontario you live. Judge the planting by how the year is progressing. In a warm year, when nights stay above freezing even early in the month, you can put in a few tender plants, such as tomatoes. If there are no more frosts, you will have gained several weeks on our short growing season. In a cool year you may even wait until after May 24 before planting to give the soil more time to warm before planting tender heat-lovers such as beans (*left*).

22

23

Start new garden beds or expand and improve old ones.

24

25

De-thatch lawns in spring only when the thatch layer is more than 2 cm (3/4") deep.

26

27

28

With their wide variety of leaf shapes, sizes and colours, hostas (left) are a popular addition to shaded Ontario gardens.

TURFGRASS

Turfgrass aficionados are having a hard time these days. Cities across Canada are taking steps to ban pesticide use on lawns, and summer water bans leave turf dry and crisp during hot spells. Alternative groundcovers and xeriscapes are being hailed as the way of the future, but there are positives to turfgrasses that make them worth keeping. Lawns efficiently filter pollutants out of run-off water, prevent soil erosion, retain moisture, cool the air and resist drought.

Although lawns require a layer of thatch to improve wear tolerance, reduce compaction and insulate against weather extremes, too thick a thatch layer can prevent water absorption, make the grass susceptible to heat, drought and cold and encourage pest and disease problems.

May-blooming flowers: (*clockwise from top*) irises bloom in early spring; forget-me-nots bloom once in spring, and flowers reappear all summer long; rockcress and phlox flowers attract bees and butterflies in spring and look exceptional in rock gardens.

29

30

31

May is the perfect time to plant such vegetables as beans, beets, leaf lettuce, peas, potatoes, radishes and spinach. They are easy to grow from seed and mature quickly.

Forget-me-nots (*left*), rockcress (*top right*) and bergenia (*bottom right*) are easy-to-grow, reliable bloomers and perfect for beginner gardeners.

Here are some tips for maintaining a healthy, organic lawn:

- Aerate your lawn in spring, after active growth begins, to relieve compaction and allow water and air to move freely through the soil.

- Feed the soil, not the plants. Organic fertilizers or compost will encourage a healthy population of soil microbes. These work with roots to provide plants with nutrients and to fight off attacks by pests and diseases. Apply an organic fertilizer in late spring after you aerate the lawn and in fall just as the grass goes dormant.

- Mow lawns to a height of 5 to 6 cm (2–2½"). If kept this height, the remaining leaf blade will shade the ground, preventing moisture loss,

keeping roots cooler, reducing the stress the grass suffers from being mowed and helping the grass out-compete weeds for space and sunlight.

- Grass clippings should be left on the lawn to return their nutrients to the soil and add organic matter. Mowing your lawn once a week or as often as needed during the vigorous growing season will ensure that the clippings decompose quickly.

- Healthy turfgrass will out-compete most weeds. Remove weeds by hand. If you must use chemicals, apply them only to the weeds. Chemical herbicides disrupt the balance of soil microbes and are not necessary to have a healthy lawn.

JUNE

*The long, warm days
of summer are with us, and the
garden flourishes.*

JUNE

Plant tender transplants such as pumpkins, tomatoes, begonias and coleus.

Heat-loving plants such as beans and marigolds will germinate quickly in the warm soil. Direct sow early in June.

Cranesbill geraniums (*left*) are charming late spring flowers with attractive foliage. The leaves of some varieties emit a lemon-mint scent.

Impatiens and ageratum (*top right*) in a tower planter; daylilies (*bottom right*) planted en masse serve as a screen.

In June, the grass is green, flower-beds are filling and perennials, trees and shrubs are blooming. We watch as seeds germinate and leaves unfold. The fear of frost is behind us, and the soil is warm enough for even the most tender plants. Rain is usually plentiful in June, but in a dry year, newly planted annuals and perennials may need supplemental watering until they become established.

THINGS TO DO

June is the month to finish up the planting and begin the general maintenance work that will keep larger projects to a minimum.

Stake plants before they fill in if you haven't already done so.

Apply mulch to shrub, perennial and vegetable beds. Doing so will shade the roots and reduce the amount of water the plants will require.

Pinch late-flowering perennials back lightly to encourage bushier growth and more flowers.

If you haven't done so already, clean out your water garden.

Remove dead flowers from plants growing in tubs, window-boxes and hanging baskets. Deadheading encourages more flowering and keeps displays looking tidy.

Prune early flowering shrubs that have finished flowering to encourage the development of young shoots that will bear flowers the following year.

Identify the insects you find in your garden. You may be surprised to find out how many are beneficial.

Despite the delicate look of its satiny flowers, godetia (*left*) enjoys the cooler weather of spring and early summer. Plants often die back as the summer progresses.

Clockwise from top right: monarda; black-eyed Susans mixed with purple coneflower; purple coneflower; artemisia; catmint

Perennials to pinch back in June:
- Artemisia (*Artemisia* species)
- Bee Balm (*Monarda didyma*)
- Black-eyed Susan (*Rudbeckia* species)
- Catmint (*Nepeta* hybrids)
- Purple Coneflower (*Echinacea purpurea*)
- Shasta Daisy (*Leucanthemum* hybrids)

Pull weeds out of beds when you see them to avoid having to spend an entire day doing it later.

Water transplants regularly until they become established.

Coreopsis (*left*) enlivens a summer garden with its bright yellow, continuous blooms. Shear back in late summer for more flowers in fall.

Clockwise from top right: abutilon in a container; charming container garden display; million bells with bidens

CONTAINER GARDENING

Most plants can be grown in containers. Annuals, perennials, vegetables, shrubs and even trees can be adapted to container culture.

There are many advantages to gardening in containers:

- They work well in small spaces. Even apartment dwellers with small balconies can enjoy the pleasures of gardening with planters on the balcony.

- They are mobile. Containers can be moved around to take advantage of light or shade and can even be moved into a sheltered location for winter.

- They are easier to reach. Container plantings allow people in wheelchairs or with back problems to garden without having to do a lot of bending.

- They are useful for extending the season. You can get an early start without the transplant shock that many plants suffer when moved outdoors. You can also protect plants from an early frost in fall.

JUNE

*Put trailing plants near the edge of
a container to spill out and bushy and
upright plants in the middle where they will
give height and depth to the planting.*

*Consider mixing different plants together in
a container. You can create contrasts of
colour, texture and habit and give a small
garden an inviting appearance.*

The flowers of *Salvia farinacea* 'Victoria' (*left*) are a
beautiful deep violet blue. They look stunning planted
with yellow or orange flowers such as nasturtiums,
California poppies or marigolds.

Clockwise from top right: marigolds, sweet potato vine
and begonias in planters; a deck improved by a vibrant
container garden; abutilon with petunias and vinca;
browallia, sweet potato vine, morning glory, dahlia and
coleus in pots.

Gardeners can get over a month's head start on the gardening season by using containers. Tomatoes, pumpkins and watermelons can be started from seed in late March. Planted into large containers, they can be moved outside during warm days and brought back in at night as needed in April and May. This prevents the stretching that many early started plants suffer from if kept indoors for too long before being planted into the garden.

Many houseplants enjoy spending the summer outside in a shady location. The brighter a location you need to provide for your plant indoors, the more likely it is to do well outdoors. Avoid putting plants in direct sun because they will have a hard time adjusting to the intensity of the light and the lack of light when they are moved back indoors at the end of the summer.

JUNE

Keep an eye open for the early signs of pest and disease problems. They are easiest to deal with when they are just beginning.

Though considered old-fashioned by some gardeners, petunias (*left*) are versatile and dependable annuals that bloom continuously in any sunny location. New varieties of this flower seem to appear every spring in Ontario greenhouses.

Spirea (*top right*) by water feature

Water gardens can be created in containers. Many ready-made container gardens are available, or you can create your own. Garden centres have lots of water garden supplies, and many water plants will grow as well in a large tub as they will in a pond.

Most perennials, shrubs or trees will require more winter protection in containers than they would if grown in the ground. Because the roots are above ground level, they are exposed to the winter wind and cycles of freezing and thawing. Protect container-grown plants by insulating the inside of the container. Thin sheets of foam insulation can be purchased and fitted around the inside of the pot before the soil is added. Containers can also be moved to sheltered locations. Garden sheds and unheated garages work well to protect plants from the cold and wind of winter.

Evergreens can be pruned once the new growth has fully extended, but while it is still tender. This new growth is called a 'candle' (*right*). Each can be pinched back by up to half to encourage bushier growth. Never cut evergreens back into old wood because most cannot regenerate from old wood.

JULY

The hot, sunny days of July encourage us
to sit back, relax and enjoy all the hard
work we've put into our gardens.

JULY

1

2

Deadhead repeat-blooming annuals and perennials regularly to keep them looking their best.

3

4

Cut flowers to use in fresh arrangements indoors.

5

6

7

The tender rose 'Ainsley Dickson' (*left*) is a reliable repeat bloomer in late summer if planted in full sun. It can produce up to 120 blossoms in its first season.

A riot of phlox, daylilies, yarrow, ageratum and snap-dragons (*top right*); a natural-looking water feature (*bottom right*)

Flowerbeds have filled in, green tomatoes ripen on the vine. The season's transplants are established and need less frequent watering. By July, the days are long, warm and humid. The garden appears to grow before your eyes. Some plants can't take the heat and fall dormant while others thrive, filling in the spaces left by the spring-flowering plants.

THINGS TO DO

Heat and drought can spell disaster for your lawn and garden if you haven't followed good watering practices. Water bans are common in communities all across Canada, and frequent, shallow watering earlier in the season makes for problems in July when roots unaccustomed to searching deeply for water suffer in its absence.

Water deeply, but no more than once a week during dry spells. Water early in the day to minimize potential disease and reduce water lost through evaporation.

Top up water gardens regularly if levels drop because of evaporation.

Thin vegetable crops such as beets, carrots and turnips. Crowded plants lead to poor crops.

Train new shoots of climbing vines such as morning glory and sweet peas to their supports.

JULY

8

9

Weed regularly to keep beds tidy.

10

11

Turn the compost pile and when the compost is ready, add it to your flowerbeds and vegetable garden.

12

13

14

Annual clary sage (*left*) loves sun, and its brilliantly coloured bracts attract butterflies and hummingbirds to the flowers. Plant it among other sun-loving annuals and perennials where its bright whites, pinks and purples will provide bright bursts of colour.

Clockwise from top right: violas; statice; bachelor's buttons

Use an organic fertilizer on container plants and on garden plants if compost is scarce.

Pick zucchini when they are small. They are tender and tasty and you are less likely to wind up with boxes full of foot-long zucchini to leave on unsuspecting neighbours' front doorsteps. Consider donating extra vegetables to a homeless shelter or food bank, where they will be much appreciated.

Plan to replace fading flowers and vegetables by sowing seeds for a fall display or crop. Peas, bush beans, annual candytuft and lobelia are often finished fruiting or blooming by mid- to late summer, leaving holes in the garden that can be filled by new plants. Seeds for replacement plants can be direct sown or started indoors.

JULY

15

16

Top mulch up if it is getting thin in places in your garden. Mulch protects roots, holds in moisture and helps keep weeds at bay.

17

18

Continue to tie plants to their stakes as they grow.

19

20

Heliopsis (*left*), a native prairie perennial, is easy to grow and tolerates poor conditions, though it thrives in full sun and fertile, moist soil. Its name means 'resembling the sun' and its sun-like blooms make long-lasting cut flowers.

Use a mixture of annuals and perennials to create garden rooms that add privacy or create paths through the garden (*opposite*).

21

An important factor in ensuring the survival of a plant in your garden is where you plant it. Find out what the best growing conditions are for your new plant to thrive, and then plant it where these conditions exist in your yard. For example, a shrub that needs full sun will never do well in a north-facing location.

GARDEN PROBLEMS

Problems such as chewed leaves, mildews and nutrient deficiencies tend to become noticeable in July when plants finish their first flush of growth and turn their attention to flowering and fruiting.

Such problems can be minimized if you develop a good problem management program. Though it may seem complicated, problem management is a simple process that relies on correct and timely identification of the problem and then using the least environmentally harmful method to deal with it.

JULY

22

23

Trim or shear back early flowering perennials when they have finished blooming.

24

25

Trim hedges regularly to keep them looking tidy and lush.

26

27

'Cupcake' (*left*) is a delightful miniature rose with a classic hybrid tea shape. It produces an abundance of blooms and is disease resistant.

Clockwise from top right: deer-pruned cedars; a swallowtail on cherry blossoms; a birdbath in a shade garden

28

Garden problems fall into three basic categories:

- pests, including insects such as aphids, nematodes and whiteflies, and animals such as mice, rabbits and deer
- diseases, caused by bacteria, fungi and viruses
- physiological problems, caused by nutrient deficiencies, too much or too little water and incorrect light levels.

Choose healthy plants that have been developed for their resistance to common problems and that will perform well in the conditions provided by your garden.

Prevention is the most important aspect of problem management. A healthy garden is resistant to problems and develops a natural balance between beneficial and detrimental organisms.

JULY

29

30

The natural pesticide pyrethrin is derived from certain species of chrysanthemums.

31

Cup-and-saucer vine (*below*) produces sweetly scented flowers that are cream coloured when they emerge and turn purple as they age.

Ladybug (*top right*), a beneficial insect that feasts on aphids; Dahlberg daisies (*bottom right*)

PEST CONTROL

Correct identification of problems is the key to solving them. Just because an insect is on a plant doesn't mean it's doing any harm.

Chemical pest control should always be a last resort. There are many alternatives that pose no danger to gardeners or their families and pets.

- Cultural controls are the day-to-day gardening techniques you use to keep your garden healthy. Weeding, mulching, keeping tools clean and growing problem-resistant cultivars are a few techniques you can use to keep gardens healthy.

- Physical controls are the hands-on part of problem solving. Picking insects off leaves, removing diseased foliage and creating barriers to stop rabbits from getting into the vegetable patch are examples of physical controls.

- Biological controls use natural and introduced populations of predators that prey on pests. Birds, snakes, frogs, spiders, some insects and even bacteria naturally feed on some problem insects. Soil microbes work with plant roots to increase their resistance to disease.

The pesticide industry has responded to consumer demand for effective, environmentally safe pest control products. Biopesticides are made from plant, animal, bacterial or mineral sources. They are effective in small quantities and decompose quickly in the environment. These products may reduce our reliance on chemical pesticides.

AUGUST

*Though the warm weather continues,
the ripening fruit, vegetables and seeds are
signs that summer is nearing its end.*

1

2

Reduce fertilizer applications to allow perennials, shrubs and trees ample time to harden off before the cold weather.

3

4

Continue to water during dry spells. Plants shouldn't need deep watering more than once a week at this time of the year.

5

6

7

Calendula (*left*) is an easy flower to grow from seed. It blooms quickly in spring and all summer long, even tolerating light frost. It can be used as a culinary herb as well.

Clockwise from top right: geraniums; deadheading asters; petunias

The hot days of July blend into August, but the nights are cooler and if it hasn't been too dry, many plants we might have given up on revive and begin a late display of colour.

THINGS TO DO

The garden seems to take care of itself in August. We gardeners putter about, tying up floppy hollyhock spikes, picking vegetables and pulling an odd weed, but the frenzy of early summer is over and we take the time just to sit and enjoy the results of our labours.

Continue to deadhead perennials and annuals to keep the blooms coming.

Remove worn-out annuals and vegetables, and replace them with the ones you started last month. Shearing some annuals and perennials back will encourage new growth, giving them a fresh look for fall.

Keep an eye open for pests that may be planning to hibernate in the debris around your plants or the bark of your trees. Taking care of a few insects now may keep several generations out of your garden next summer.

Pick apples as soon as they are ready, being careful not to bruise the fruit.

AUGUST

8

9

Seed areas of the lawn that are thin or dead. Keep the seed well watered while it germinates.

10

11

Depending on the size of your perennials, you can divide them using a shovel or pitchfork (for large plants), a sharp knife (for small plants) or your hands (for easily divided plants).

12

13

14

The French marigold (*left*) is just one variety of this popular annual. All marigolds are low-maintenance plants that stand up well to heat, wind and rain.

PLANT PROPAGATION

Now is a good time to divide some perennials and to note which of your plants will need dividing next spring. Look for these signs that perennials need dividing:

- The centre of the plant has died out.
- The plant is no longer flowering as profusely as it did in previous years.
- The plant is encroaching on the growing space of other plants.

August is a good time to propagate plants. Taking cuttings and gathering seed are great ways to increase your plant collection and to share some of your favourite plants with friends and family.

Plants such as Siberian bugloss (top), anemone (top right), liatrus (centre) and penstemon (right) are good plants to divide if you're just starting your perennial collection. They recover and fill in quickly when divided.

15

16

Gradually move houseplants that have been summering outdoors into shadier locations so they will be prepared for the lower light levels indoors. Make sure they aren't infested with bugs; the pests will be harder to control once the plants are indoors.

17

18

Turn the layers of the compost pile and continue to add garden soil, kitchen scraps and garden debris that isn't diseased or infested with insects.

19

20

Zinnias (*below*) are easy to grow, come in a rainbow of colours and make long-lasting cut flowers for floral arrangements.

Clockwise from top right: basket-of-gold, sedum and aster are easy to propagate from stem cuttings.

21

Perennials, trees, shrubs and tender perennials that are treated like annuals can all be started from cuttings. This method is an excellent way to propagate varieties and cultivars that you really like but that are slow or difficult to start from seed or that don't produce viable seed.

The easiest cuttings to take from woody plants such as trees, shrubs and vines are called semi-ripe, semi-mature or semi-hardwood cuttings. They are taken from mature new growth that has not become completely woody yet, usually in late summer or early fall.

There is some debate over what size cuttings should be. Some claim that smaller cuttings are more likely to root and will root more quickly. Others claim that larger cuttings develop more roots and become established more quickly once planted. Try different sizes and see what works best for you.

AUGUST

*Continue watering newly planted
perennials, trees and shrubs.
Water deeply to encourage root growth.*

*Avoid pruning rust-prone plants
such as mountain ash and crabapple in
late summer and fall because many rusts
are releasing spores now.*

You won't need to collect seed from
borage (*left*) because these plants self-
seed profusely and will no doubt turn
up in your garden next spring.

Clockwise from top right: evening
primrose; nasturtiums with creeping
Jenny; zinnias

The easiest way to start is to collect seeds of annual plants in your own garden. Choose plants that are not hybrids or the seeds will probably not come true to type and may not germinate at all. A few easy plants to collect from are

- Borage (*Borago officinalis*)
- Calendula (*Calendula officinalis*)
- Coriander (*Coriandrum sativum*)
- Evening Primrose (*Oenothera biennis*)
- Fennel (*Foeniculum vulgare*)
- Marigold (*Tagetes* species and hybrids)
- Nasturtium (*Tropaeolum majus*)
- Poppy (*Papaver rhoeas*)
- Zinnia (*Zinnia elegans*)

Always make cuttings just below a leaf node, the point where the leaves are attached to the stem.

Many gardeners enjoy the hobby of collecting and planting seed. You need to know a few basic things before you begin:

- Know your plant. Correctly identify the plant and learn about its life cycle. You will need to know when it flowers, when the seeds are likely to ripen and how the plant disperses its seeds in order to collect them.
- Find out if there are special requirements for starting the seeds. For example, do they need a hot or cold period to germinate?

AUGUST

29

30

*Find a source of straw for mulch
now because it can be harder
to find later in fall.*

31

Nasturtiums (*below*) are versatile annuals. Their
edible flowers and foliage are attractive additions to
baskets and containers as well as to salads. Even the
seedpods can be pickled and used as a substitute
for capers.

Clockwise from top right: drying poppy seedheads;
Oriental poppy; golden clematis flowers
and seedheads

When collecting seed, consider the following:

- Collect seeds once they are ripe but before they are shed from the parent plant.

- Remove capsules, heads or pods as they begin to dry and remove the seeds later, once they are completely dry.

- Place a paper bag over a seed-head as it matures and loosely tie it in place to collect seeds as they are shed.

- Dry seeds after they've been collected. Place them on a paper-lined tray and leave them in a warm, dry location for one to three weeks.

- Separate seeds from the other plant parts before storing.

- Store seeds in air-tight containers in a cool, frost-free location.

Don't collect seeds from the wild because wild harvesting is severly depleting many plant populations. Many species and populations of wild plants are protected, and it is illegal to collect their seeds.

Collecting and saving seeds is a time-honoured tradition. Early settlers brought seeds with them when they came to North America and saved them carefully each fall for the following spring.

SEPTEMBER

Though we cling tenaciously to any summer weather that lingers, there's no denying that fall is upon us.

SEPTEMBER

1

2

*Pull out annual plants and vegetables
as they fade or are killed by frost.*

3

4

*Plant colourful fall ornamentals, such
as chrysanthemums, flowering cabbage
and flowering kale, available in
fall at most garden centres.*

5

6

7

Goldenrod (*left*), amaranthus (*top right*), strawflower
(*centre right*) and nigella (*bottom right*) can be harvested now for dried flower arrangements.

Leaves begin to change colour, ripening seedheads nod in the breeze and brightly coloured berries and fruit adorn many trees and shrubs. There is a strong likelihood of frost before the end of September for northern gardens while summer sometimes seems never-ending in the south. Many annuals are undamaged by early frosts and continue to bloom until the first hard freeze.

THINGS TO DO

Having enjoyed another summer garden, your big fall clean-up begins.

Take advantage of end-of-season sales. Many garden centres are getting rid of trees, shrubs and perennials at reduced prices. There is still plenty of time for the roots to become established before the ground freezes. Do not buy plants that are excessively pot bound.

Consider starting some herb seeds now. You can plant them in pots and keep them in a bright window so you'll have fresh herbs to add to soups and salads over winter. Moving herb plants in from outdoors is also possible, but the plants often have a difficult time adapting to the lower light levels indoors.

SEPTEMBER

8

9

Dig up tuberous tender plants such as begonias for drying and storing over winter.

10

11

Continue to water the garden during dry spells. Consistent watering in fall helps prepare plants for winter.

12

13

Lilies (*left*) are long-lived, easy-to-grow perennials. They look superb in floral arrangements combined with flowers such as baby's breath (*left*).

Clockwise from top left: the fall colours and features of Virginia creeper, burning bush, full moon maple and ginkgo

14

If you've let your weeds get out of hand over summer, be sure to pull them up before they set seed to avoid having even more weeds popping up in the garden next summer.

Cool fall weather is ideal for sowing grass seed and repairing thin patches in the lawn.

The changing colours are a sure sign that fall is here. Bright reds, golds, bronzes and coppers seem to give warmth to a cool day. The display doesn't have to be reserved for a walk in the park. Include trees and shrubs with good fall colour such as the ones listed here to your garden:

- Maples (*Acer*)
- Burning Bush (*Euonymus alatus*)
- Virginia Creeper (*Parthenocissus quinquefolia*)
- Cotoneaster (*Cotoneaster*)
- Witch-hazel (*Hamamelis*)

SEPTEMBER

15

16

*Set up birdfeeders and begin to feed
the birds if you didn't do so all summer.*

17

*Move tender container plants into a
sheltered location when frost is
expected. This strategy will allow you
to enjoy them for longer.*

18

19

20

The cheery golden marguerite daisy plant (*below*)
forms a tidy mound that works wonderfully in both
formal and informal garden settings.

Clockwise from top right: primroses; tulips, bluebells
and candytuft; alliums; rudbeckia (black-eyed Susan)

21

❦

Begin to plant bulbs for a great display next spring. Tulips, daffodils, crocuses, scillas, muscaris and alliums are just a few of the bulbs whose flowers will welcome you back into the garden next year.

❦

Spring-flowering perennials such as primroses and candytuft will be a delightful sight come April and May and can be planted now.

❦

For vivacious colour from summer through fall, a continuous blooming perennial such as rudbeckia can't be beat.

SEPTEMBER

22

23

When planting bulbs, you may want to add a little bonemeal to the soil to encourage root development.

24

25

Check houseplants for insect pests before moving them back indoors for winter.

26

27

Echinacea purpurea (*left*), commonly called purple coneflower and used as a popular herbal cold remedy, is a long-blooming, drought-resistant perennial. Its distinctively cone-shaped flowers look good in fresh and dried floral arrangements.

Opposite page: Garden features such as birdbaths, bird-feeders and tall flowering perennials such as beebalm, coneflower and yarrow attract wildlife to your yard.

28

CREATING WILDLIFE HABITAT

The rapid rate of urban sprawl has led to the relentless expansion of large cities and a loss of habitat for wildlife. Our gardens can easily provide some of the space, shelter, food and water that wildlife needs. Though we may not want to attract every creature, we can make at least some wildlife welcome in our gardens. Here are a few tips for attracting wildlife to your garden:

- Make sure at least some of the plants in your garden are locally native. Birds and small animals are accustomed to certain plants for food. These plants will attract the wildlife to your garden, where it may be tempted to try some of the other fruit that is not native.

- Provide a source of water. A pond with a shallow side or a birdbath will offer water for drinking and bathing. Frogs and toads eat a wide variety of insect pests and will happily take up residence in or near a ground-level water feature.

- A variety of birdfeeders and seed will encourage different species of birds to visit your garden. Some birds will visit an elevated feeder, but others prefer a feeder set at or near ground level. Fill your feeders regularly—once you start to feed the birds, they will come to depend on you as a source of food.

29   30

The zinnia (*below*) is named after Johann Gottfried Zinn (1727–59), a German botany professor who started growing these South American flowers from seed in Europe.

Clockwise from top right: birdfeeder; monarda with butterfly; sunflower; maple tree

- Butterflies, hummingbirds and a wide variety of predatory insects will be attracted if you include lots of pollen-producing plants in your garden. Plants such as goldenrod, comfrey, bee balm, salvia, Joe-Pye weed, black-eyed Susan, catmint, purple coneflower, coreopsis, hollyhock and yarrow will attract pollen lovers.

- Shelter is the final aspect to keeping your resident wildlife happy. Patches of dense shrubs, tall grasses and mature trees provide shelter. As well, you can leave a small pile of twiggy brush in an out-of-the-way place. Nature stores and many garden centres sell toad houses and birdhouses.

Inevitably squirrels and chipmunks will try to get at your birdfeeders. In areas where squirrels are not a problem, instead of trying to get rid of them, why not leave peanuts and seeds out for them as well? Place them near a tree, where they can easily get at them. If you have a large spruce tree, they will eat the seeds out of the cones. Leave cones out with the other food offerings. The little cone scales that are left when they are done make great mulch for the garden or can be used to prevent slipping on icy walks and driveways.

OCTOBER

This month marks the inevitable end
of summer. Frosts and falling leaves
remind us that winter is not far off.

OCTOBER

1

2

Continue to plant bulbs. They need to get a bit of root growth in fall in order to flower next spring.

3

4

Continue to mow the lawn, but don't mow frozen blades of grass. Wait for frost to melt off and dry before cutting the grass.

5

6

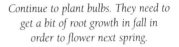

7

If the first frost hasn't yet arrived and your apples are still on the tree (left), now is the time to harvest them. However, some varieties taste better after the first frost.

Clockwise from top right: a fall wreath can be made from garden clippings; a bountiful harvest of carrots; endearing teddy bear sunflowers

The garden may still be vigorous early in the month, but by Halloween, only the hardy bloomers may still be going strong. Though we may wake up some mornings to a frost-dusted world, we continue to enjoy warm days for most of the month. Some years, an early fall of snow gives children a chance to make a snowman on the lawn.

THINGS TO DO

October is the time to finish tidying up and putting the garden to bed for another year.

Harvest any remaining vegetables. Soft fruit such as tomatoes and zucchini should be harvested before the first frost, but cool weather vegetables such as carrots, cabbage, brussels sprouts and turnips can wait a while longer because they are frost hardy.

Unless your plants have been afflicted with some sort of disease, you can leave faded perennial growth in place and clean it up in spring. The stems will collect leaves and snow, protecting the roots and crown of the plant over the winter.

OCTOBER

8

9

Continue to tidy up dead plant material. Most can be composted, but diseased material is better thrown out.

10

11

Start mulching the garden, but avoid covering plants completely until the ground has frozen. Doing so prevents plants from rotting and deters small rodents from digging down and feasting on plant roots and crowns.

12

13

14

The serviceberry (*left*) is a small tree that bears white flowers and edible red berries in spring and lovely orange-red foliage in fall. It requires little maintenance and does quite well near water.

Fall is a great time to improve your soil. Amendments added now can be worked in lightly. By planting time next spring, the amendments will have been further worked in by the actions of worms and other soil microorganisms and by the freezing and thawing that takes place over winter.

When raking leaves up in fall, you can use them in different ways: add them to the compost pile; gather them into their own compost pile to decompose into leaf mould; or mow them over and then pile them onto flowerbeds. Whole leaves can become matted together, encouraging fungal disease.

Local farmers' markets are often the best places to find a wide variety of seasonal vegetables and flowers (*above and below*).

OCTOBER

15

16

Continue to water trees and shrubs
until freeze up. Apply an organic
anti-desiccant to newly planted evergreens
to reduce winter moisture loss.

17

18

Faded annuals and vegetables can be pulled
up and added to the compost pile.

19

20

21

Honeysuckle vine (*left*) flowers from summer to fall
frost. Prune in spring to cut back dead growth as
new leaves emerge.

Composting (*far right*); delicious vegetables
harvested from the garden (*near right*)

COMPOSTING

One of the best additives for any type of soil is compost. Compost can be purchased at most garden centres, and many communities now have composting programs. You can easily make compost in your own garden. Though garden refuse and vegetable scraps from your kitchen left in a pile will eventually decompose, it is possible to produce compost more quickly. Here are a few suggestions for creating compost:

▪ Compost decomposes most quickly when there is a balance between dry and fresh materials. There should be more dry matter, such as chopped straw or shredded leaves, than green matter, such as vegetable scraps and grass clippings.

▪ Layer the dry and the green matter and mix in some garden soil or previously finished compost. This step introduces decomposer organisms to the pile.

OCTOBER

As outdoor gardening winds down,
try starting bulbs such as paperwhites
(narcissus) indoors. Fragrant white blooms
should emerge in a few weeks.

Cure winter squash, such as pumpkins,
acorn squash and spaghetti squash,
in a cool, frost-free location before
storing for winter.

Yarrow's showy, flat-topped flowerheads (*left*) provide months of
continuous colour in summer and the
seedheads persist into winter.

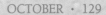

■ Compost won't decompose properly if it is too wet or too dry. Keep the pile covered during heavy rain and sprinkle it with water if it is too dry. The correct level of moisture can best be described as that of a wrung-out sponge.

■ To aerate the pile, use a garden fork to poke holes in it or turn it regularly. Use a thermometer with a long probe attached, similar to a large meat thermometer, to check the temperature in your pile. When the temperature reaches 70° C, give the pile a turn.

■ Finished compost is dark in colour and light in texture. When you can no longer recognize what went into the compost, it is ready for use.

■ Compost can be mixed into garden soil or spread on the surface as a mulch.

Images of fall: ripe pumpkins (*top left*); juicy clusters of vine-ripened grapes (*top*); tasty corn on the cob fresh from the garden (*above*). Many gardeners find fruiting plants to be decorative as well as useful.

OCTOBER

29

30

If you haven't got the time or the inclination to fuss over your compost, you can just leave it in a pile and it will eventually decompose with no added assistance from you.

31

Sunflowers (*below*) are synonymous with fall for many gardeners. Their bold yellow, seed-filled flowerheads celebrate the harvest season and provide treats for the birds.

Viburnum's fall berries (*right*) attract birds and can be used to make jellies, pies and wine.

Before adding any amendments to your soil, you should get a soil test done. Simple kits to test for pH and major nutrients are available at garden centres. More thorough tests are done at government or private labs. These tests will tell you what the pH is, the comparative levels of sand, silt, clay and organic matter and the quantities of all required nutrients. They will also tell you what amendments to add and in what quantities to improve your soil.

There are other good amendments for soil, depending on what is required:

- Gypsum can be mixed into a clay soil along with compost to loosen the structure and allow water to penetrate.
- Elemental sulphur, peat moss or pine needles added on a regular basis can make an alkaline soil more acidic.
- Calcitic or dolomitic limestone, hydrated lime, quicklime or wood ashes can be added to an acidic soil to make it more alkaline.

Sunflowers (*above*) and other cut flowers can be found in abundance in farmers' markets throughout the province. Use them for fresh or dried table arrangements, or flower pressing for winter crafts.

NOVEMBER

Branches lie bare, dry flowerheads sway in the breeze and excited birds pick brightly coloured fruit from frost-covered branches.

NOVEMBER

1

2

After raking and once the lawn is dormant, apply an organic fertilizer. If you haven't needed to mow in a couple of weeks, it is probably sufficiently dormant.

3

4

If you have healthy willows, dogwoods, Virginia creeper or evergreens, cut a few branches to use in Christmas wreaths. Store in a cool place until needed.

5

6

7

Annual coreopsis (left) self-seeds, so it may pop up from year to year in the same area if left to its own devices.

Despite the inevitable frosts, a few stragglers always hang on. Flowers like calendula keep blooming, even under a light blanket of snow, until the ground starts to freeze. The ground may freeze by mid-month in the north but doesn't until December in most Ontario gardens.

THINGS TO DO

Garden tasks this month centre around finishing tucking the garden in for winter.

Harvest any remaining vegetables. Root vegetables, such as carrots, parsnips and turnips, and green vegetables, such as cabbages and broccoli, store well in a cool place, and their flavour is often improved after a touch of frost.

The garden can be quite beautiful in November, especially when persistent fruit becomes more visible on branches (*below*) or after a light dusting of snow or frost (*right*).

NOVEMBER

8

9

Clear away tools, hoses and garden furniture
before the snow flies so they won't be
damaged by the cold and wet weather.

10

11

Mound mulch around the bases of semi-
hardy shrubs once the ground freezes
to protect the roots and stem bases
from temperature fluctuations.

12

13

The beautiful hybrid tea rose 'Rosemary Harkness'
(*left*) produces fragrant orange-yellow double
blooms from summer to autumn. Like other tender
hybrid teas, it should be protected from Ontario's
often harsh winter weather.

The richly coloured rosettes of ornamental kale
(*far right*) are reminiscent of roses (*top right*);
strawberry (*centre right*); colourful fall maple leaves
(*bottom right*)

14

Prepare hybrid tea and other semi-hardy roses for before the ground freezes. Mound dirt up over the base and cover with mulch, or cover it with a cardboard box, open the top and fill around the plant with loose, quick-drying material, such as sawdust, shredded leaves or peat moss. Hold the box in place with a heavy rock on top when you are done.

Avoid completely covering perennials with mulch until the ground freezes. Mound the mulch around them (*above*) and store some extra mulch in a frost-free location to add once they are frozen. If you pile the mulch in the garden, you may find it has also frozen solid when you want to use it.

NOVEMBER

15

16

Be sure to enjoy any remaining warm days before the garden becomes the dream of next summer.

17

18

Fill your birdfeeders regularly. Well-fed birds will continue to visit your garden in summer, feeding on undesirable insects in your garden.

19

20

Pieris (*left*) is a beautiful plant all year long. It provides colourful new growth in spring and summer and flowers from late winter to mid spring.

Clockwise from top right: hollyhock; hens and chicks; jack pine; lilac

21

If an area of your garden always seems dry, consider a xeriscape planting in that area. Many plants are drought resistant and thrive even in areas that are never watered. Yarrow, hollyhock, prickly pear cactus, black-eyed Susan, jack pine, potentilla, lilac and cosmos are just a few of the many possibilities for a dry section of the garden.

Now that you've had the chance to observe your garden for a growing season, consider the microclimates and think about how you can put them to good use. Are any always quick to dry? Do some areas stay wet longer than others? What area is the most sheltered? Which is the least sheltered? Cater your plantings to the microclimates of your garden.

NOVEMBER

22

23

Wait for the ground to freeze up before covering or wrapping tender shrubs and evergreens to ensure that all growth has slowed for winter.

24

25

Spray anti-desiccants on evergreens, such as rhododendrons and cedars, to prevent moisture loss over winter.

26

27

28

Flowers such as marsh marigolds (*left*), irises (*top and far right*), daylilies (*centre right*) and ligularia (*bottom right*) work well in damp areas of the garden because they prefer moist growing conditions.

BOG GARDENING

Turn a damp area into your own little bog garden. Dig out a damp area 35–50 cm (14–20") below ground level, line with a piece of punctured pond liner and fill with soil. The area will stay wet but still allow some water to drain away, providing a perfect location to plant moisture-loving perennials. A few to consider are

- Astilbe (*Astilbe* x *arendsii*)
- Cardinal Flower (*Lobelia* x *speciosa*)
- Daylily (*Hemerocallis* hybrids)
- Doronicum (*Doronicum orientale*)
- Goatsbeard (*Aruncus dioicus*)
- Hosta (*Hosta* hybrids)
- Iris (*Iris ensata, Iris siberica*)
- Lady's Mantle (*Alchemilla mollis*)
- Ligularia (*Ligularia dentata* and *wilsoniana*)
- Marsh Marigold (*Caltha palustris*)
- Meadowsweet (*Filipendula rubra* and *ulmaria*)
- Primrose (*Primula japonica*)
- Rodgersia (*Rodgersia aesculifolia*)

Finish collecting seeds from open-pollinated flowers and vegetables. Stored in a cool, dry place, they will be ready for planting in next year's garden.

Oregon grape holly (*near right*); caryopteris (*far right*); pieris (*bottom right*)

Rodgersia (*left*) bears bold foliage and fluffy flower plumes in mid- to late summer. It does best in a site sheltered from strong winds and extreme weather. Rodgersia plants prefer moist soil and require winter protection in colder Ontario gardens.

It is possible to grow out-of-zone plants. Reserve the warmest, most sheltered area of the garden for plants not considered fully hardy. Pieris, Oregon grapeholly and caryopteris may survive in a suitably sheltered location.

If you have a very exposed area in your garden, you can find plants that will do well there, or you can make a planting that will shelter the area. A hedge (*centre right*) or group of trees or shrubs will break the wind and provide an attractive feature for your garden.

DECEMBER

*Already summer seems far away. Ghostly
forms and dashes of colour are all that
remain to inspire us until spring.*

DECEMBER

1

2

*If you haven't already done so,
finish mulching the garden.*

3

4

*Clean tools thoroughly and wipe them
with an oily rag to prevent them from
rusting before storing them for winter.*

5

6

7

Holly (*left*) makes an attractive addition to fresh
winter arrangements. To keep it looking its best,
keep the cut ends consistently moist.

The garden begins its winter display of colourful and peeling bark, branches with persistent fruit and evergreen boughs. With a bit of luck, snow begins to pile up on garden beds, covering withered perennials and shrubs and clinging to evergreen branches. Winter arrives, hopefully in time for the holidays, driving away our fond memories of the garden.

THINGS TO DO

Our thoughts turn to indoor gardening though we may still have a few garden tasks to complete before we call it a year.

Gently brush snow off flexible evergreen branches. Heavy snow can weigh down upright juniper and cedar branches enough to permanently bend them downwards.

Water evergreens and shrubs thoroughly before the ground freezes. They won't have any access to water again until the ground thaws in spring.

If rabbits and mice are a problem in your garden, you can protect your trees and shrubs with chicken wire. Wrap it around the plant bases and higher up the tree or shrub than you expect the snow to reach.

In December our thoughts turn to decorating for the holidays. Now is the time to use some of the flowers you dried to make potpourri, wreaths or floral arrangements (*above and left*).

8

9

Move clay and concrete pots and statues into a protected location to prevent them from cracking over winter.

10

11

Reduce watering and cease feeding houseplants.

12

13

14

Poinsettias (*left*) add rich colour and beauty to our homes during the dark days of December.

Clockwise from top right: ficus (weeping fig); *Cattleya* orchid; *Miltonopsis* orchid; cast iron plant

HOUSEPLANT CARE

You don't have to forget gardening completely when the snow begins to fly. All you have to do is turn your attention to indoor gardening. Houseplants clean the air, soften the hard edges of a room and provide colour, texture and interest to your home.

Just as you did for the garden outdoors, match your indoor plants to the conditions your home provides. If a room receives little light, consider houseplants that require very low light levels. Plants that like humid conditions may do best in your bathroom where showering and the toilet bowl full of water maintain higher moisture levels than in any other room. Low-light-tolerant plants include philodendron, cast iron plant and snake plant. Bright-light-tolerant plants include cacti, jade plant and goldfish plant.

DECEMBER

15

16

Most indoor plant pests can be controlled by wiping leaves with a damp sponge. More difficult pests can be controlled with insecticidal soap.

17

18

Any herbs you are growing indoors should be kept in the brightest window you have to prevent them from becoming too straggly or dying.

19

20

Although orchids are reputed to be difficult and needy, some orchids such as the moth orchid *Phalaenopsis* (*left*) are easy to grow on a windowsill. There are many thousands of species of orchids in an amazing array of sizes, shapes, colours and fragrances.

Indoor water garden (*centre right*); braided lucky bamboo (*bottom right*)

21

There are three aspects of interior light to consider: intensity, duration and quality. Intensity is the difference between a south-facing window with full sun and a north-facing room with no direct sunlight. Duration is how long the light lasts in a specific location. An east-facing window will have a shorter duration of light than a south-facing window. Quality refers to the spectrum of the light. Natural light provides a broader spectrum than artificial light.

Watering is a key element to houseplant care. Over-watering can be as much of a problem as under-watering. As you did with your garden plants, water thoroughly and infrequently. Let the soil dry out a bit before watering plants. Some plants are the exception to this rule. Find out what the water requirements of your houseplants are so you will have an idea of how frequently or infrequently you will need to water.

Look for creative ways to display your plants and add beauty to your home. Indoor fountains and moisture-loving plants, such as a peace lily, in a vase of water (*top*) are interesting and attractive to look at. They add a decorative touch to a houseplant display.

DECEMBER

22

23

*Dust on plants is more than just an eyesore.
It prevents plants from making full use
of the light they receive. Clean leaves
regularly with a damp cloth or sponge,
or place them in the shower and let
the water stream wash away any dust.*

24

25

*Ice storms are a strong possibility for many
Ontario gardeners. Though the sunlight
glinting off ice-covered branches is beautiful,
the ice can be very damaging to plants.
Breaking it off can do a lot of damage,
so it is better to let it melt naturally.*

26

27

28

English ivy (*left*) that you've grown outdoors
all summer can be brought indoors and kept
as a houseplant in winter.

An interesting houseplant display (*top right*);
snake plant (*bottom right*), a striking, long-lived
indoor plant

Houseplants generally only need fertilizer when they are actively growing. Always use a weak fertilizer to avoid burning the roots. Never feed plants when they are very dry. Moisten the soil by watering and then feed a couple of days later.

When repotting, go up by only one size at a time. In general the new pot should be no more than 5–10 cm (2–4") larger in diameter than the previous pot. If you find your soil drying out too frequently, then you may wish to use a larger pot that will stay moist for longer.

Houseplants are more than just attractive—they clean the air in our homes. Many dangerous and common toxins, such as benzene, formaldehyde and trichloroethylene are absorbed and eliminated by houseplants.

Here are a few easy-to-grow, toxin-absorbing houseplants:

- Spider Plant (*Chlorophytum cosmosum*)
- Peace Lily (*Spathiphyllum* 'Mauna Loa')
- Bamboo Palm (*Camaedorea erumpens*)
- Pot Mum (*Chrysanthemum morifolium*)
- English Ivy (*Hedera helix*)
- Weeping Fig (*Ficus benjamina*)
- Chinese Evergreen (*Aglaonema modestum*)
- Dragon Tree (*Dracaena marginata*)
- Snake Plant (*Sansevieria trifasciata*)
- Gerbera Daisy (*Gerbera jamesonii*)

DECEMBER

29

Plants can be grouped together in large containers to more easily meet the needs of the plants. Cacti can be planted together in a gritty soil mix and placed in a dry, bright location. Moisture and humidity-loving plants can be planted in a large terrarium where moisture levels remain higher.

30

31

A bouquet of cheerful gerberas (*below*) will brighten a drab winter day and remind you of summer, when these flowers were growing in your garden.

Cacti (*near right*) make good houseplants because they are undemanding and tolerate the dry air found in most homes quite well.

Keep in mind that many common houseplants are tropical and dislike hot, dry conditions. Most house-plants will thrive in cooler, moister conditions than you will provide in your home. Always turn thermo-stats down at night and provide moist conditions by sitting pots on pebble trays. Water in the pebble tray can evaporate but won't soak excessively into the soil of the pot because the pebbles hold it above the water.

There's nothing like treating yourself to a bouquet of fresh flowers (*above*) when you're feeling the doldrums of winter. Many beautiful varieties are available. Watch for some of the more exotic plants from South America and Australia at grocery stores and florist shops.

RESOURCES

Books

Armitage, Allan M. 2000. *Armitage's Garden Perennials*. Timber Press, Portland, OR.

Beck, Alison and Kathy Renwald. 2001. *Annuals for Ontario*. Lone Pine Publishing, Edmonton, AB.

——. 2001. *Tree & Shrub Gardening for Ontario*. Lone Pine Publishing, Edmonton, AB.

——. 2001. *Perennials for Ontario*. Lone Pine Publishing, Edmonton, AB.

Bezener, Andy. 2000. *Birds of Ontario*. Lone Pine Publishing, Edmonton, AB.

Brickell, Christopher., T.J. Cole and J.D. Zuk, eds. 1996. *Reader's Digest A–Z Encyclopedia of Garden Plants*. The Reader's Digest Association Ltd., Montreal, PQ.

Brickell, Christopher and David Joyce. 1996. *Pruning and Training*. Dorling Kindersley Limited, London, England.

Bubel, Nancy. 1988. *The New Seed Starter's Handbook*. Rodale Press, Emmaus, PA.

Casselman, Bill. 1997. *Canadian Garden Words*. Little, Brown and Company (Canada) Ltd., Toronto, ON.

Courtier, Jane and Graham Clarke. 1997. *Indoor Plants: The Essential Guide to Choosing and Caring for Houseplants*. Reader's Digest, Westmount, PQ.

Dirr, Michael A. 1997. *Dirr's Hardy Trees and Shrubs*. Timber Press, Portland, OR.

Ellis, B.W. and F.M. Bradley, eds. 1996. *The Organic Gardener's Handbook of Natural Insect and Disease Control*. Rodale Press, Emmaus, PA.

Heintzelman, Donald S. 2001. *The Complete Backyard Birdwatcher's Home Companion*. Ragged Mountain Press, Camden, ME.

Hole, Lois. 1993. *Lois Hole's Vegetable Favorites*. Lone Pine Publishing, Edmonton, AB.

——. 1994. *Lois Hole's Bedding Plant Favorites*. Lone Pine Publishing, Edmonton, AB.

——. 1995. *Lois Hole's Perennial Favorites*. Lone Pine Publishing, Edmonton, AB.

——. 1996. *Lois Hole's Tomato Favorites*. Lone Pine Publishing, Edmonton, AB.

——. 1997. *Lois Hole's Rose Favorites*. Lone Pine Publishing, Edmonton, AB.

——. 1997. *Lois Hole's Favorite Trees and Shrubs*. Lone Pine Publishing, Edmonton, AB.

Hill, Lewis. 1991. *Secrets of Plant Propagation*. Storey Communications Inc., Pownal, VT.

Kershaw, Linda. 2002. *Ontario Wildflowers*. Lone Pine Publishing, Edmonton, AB.

McHoy, Peter. 2002. *Houseplants*. Hermes House, New York, NY.

McVicar, Jekka. 1997. *Jekka's Complete Herb Book*. Raincoast, Vancouver, BC.

Merilees, Bill. 1989. *Attracting Backyard Wildlife: A Guide for Nature Lovers*. Voyageur Press, Stillwater, MN.

Peters, Laura and Liz Klose. 2003. *Roses for Ontario*. Lone Pine Publishing, Edmonton, AB.

Robinson, Peter. 1997. *Complete Guide to Water Gardening*. Reader's Digest, Westmount, PQ.

Thompson, P. 1992. *Creative Propagation: A Grower's Guide*. Timber Press, Portland, OR.

Online Resources

Agriculture and Agri-Food Canada. Climate information for Ontario. www.agr.gc.ca/index_e.phtml

Aquatics & Co. Comprehensive water gardening information and products. www.aquaticsco.com

Attracting Wildlife to your yard.com. How to make your backyard inviting to compatible and beneficial creatures. www.attracting-wildlife-to-your-garden.com

Backyard Gardener. Offers gardening information, a newsletter, articles and online shopping. www.backyardgardener.com

Botanique.com. Offers a listing of the botanical gardens in Ontario. www.botanique.com

Butterfly Website. Learn about the fascinating world of butterflies. www.butterflywebsite.com

Canadian Gardening. Ask the expert section and an extensive listing of gardening catalogues. www.canadiangardening.com/home.html

Canadian Organic Growers. Contains fantastic information on organic growing. www.cog.ca

Canadian Wildlife Federation. Everything you wanted to know about attracting wildlife. www.cwf-fcf.org/pages/indexe.htm

Centre Commons Perennials. Among other things, this website offers a lengthy list of Ontario horticultural societies. www.centrecommons.com e-mail: kcarriere@centrecommons.com

City of Toronto. Simple and thorough information on growing a healthy lawn without chemicals. www.city.toronto.on.ca/parks/healthy-lawn/index.htm

Civic Garden Centre at Edwards Gardens. Information, courses and more. www.civicgardencentre.org e-mail: civicgardencentre@infogarden.ca

Composting Council of Canada. A national non-profit organization that encourages composting. www.compost.org

Evergreen Foundation. A national environmental organization that provides tools to transform residential and commercial spaces into healthy outdoor spaces. www.evergreen.ca/en/index.html

Gardenimport Inc. Specializes in bulbs. www.gardenimport.com

I Can Garden. Information and a gardening forum where you can contact gardeners from across Canada and the world. www.icangarden.com/

Landscape Ontario and the Horticultural Trades Association. Information on landscaping in Ontario and recommendations for landscapers and designers. www.landscapeontario.com

North American Native Plant Society. Dedicated to the study, conservation and restoration of native plants. www.nanps.org/index.shtml

Ontario Gardening. Comprehensive information about gardening in Ontario. www.ontariogardening.com

Northern Gardening Forum. List of gardening forums intended for northern U.S. but used by many Canadians.
www.northerngardening.com/
cgi-bin/ultimatebb.cgi

Organic Gardening–Canada.
Information and resources for gardening organically.www.coab.ca/gardening.htm

Pickering Nurseries Inc. Over 800 varieties of roses available by mail order.
www.pickeringnurseries.com

Richters. The best Canadian herb resource for information and sales.
www.richters.com

Seeds of Diversity Canada. A group of gardeners that save and share seeds of rare, unusual and heritage plants.
www.seeds.ca/en.htm

Turf Resource Center and The Lawn Institute. The latest data on turfgrass.
www.TurfGrassSod.org
www.LawnInstitute.com

University of Illinois Extension.
Information on houseplant care, annuals, perennials, growing vegetables and fruit, diseases and insects, herbs and seasonal features.
www.urbanext.uiuc.edu/houseplants/

Urban Agriculture Notes by City Farmer.
Great ideas from around the world to involve children in the family garden.
www.cityfarmer.org/schgard15.html

Virtual Gardener. An online magazine based on organic principles.
www.gardenmag.com

Soil-Testing Facilities

A & L Canada Laboratories East, Inc.
2136 Jetstream Road
London, ON N5V 3P5
519–457–2575
www.alcanada.com

Accutest Laboratories
146 Colonnade Road, Unit #8
Nepean, ON K2E 7Y1
613–727–5692
www.accutestlabs.com

Laboratory Services (a division of the University of Guelph)
95 Stone Road W, Guelph, ON
N1H 8J7
519–767–6226
www.uoguelph.ca/labserv/
e-mail: info@lsd.uoguelph.ca

Nutrite
Box 160, Elmira, ON N3B 2Z6
519–669–5401

Horticultural Societies

The Ontario Horticultural Association
1807 Orr Road
Mississauga, ON L5J 1B8
www.interlog.com/~onthort/
e-mail: bonnie@ntl.sympatico.ca
(Contact: Bonnie Warner)
Offers information about the 19 districts and 278 gardening clubs and horticultural societies throughout Ontario.

The Ottawa Botanical Garden Society
Box 727, Postal Station "B"
59 Sparks St., Ottawa, ON K1P 5P8
819–291–2820
www.ottawagarden.ca
e-mail: obgs@magma.ca

Gardens to Visit

Allan Botanical Gardens
19 Horticultural Ave., between Gerard and Jarvis, Toronto, ON
416–392–1111
www.city.toronto.on.ca http://
collections.ic.gc.ca./gardens/

Arboretum and Gardens at the University of Guelph
Arboretum Road between College Ave. E and Stone Rd. E, Guelph, ON
519–824–4120 ext. 2113
www.uoguelph.ca

Brickman's Botanical Gardens
RR1 Sebringville
Sebringville (Wartburg), ON
519–393–6223
www.brickmansbotanicalgardens.com
e-mail: brickmans@quadro.net

Centennial Botanical Conservatory
1601 Dease St., Thunder Bay, ON
807–625–2351

Edward Gardens
777 Lawrence Ave. E, Toronto, ON
416–397–8186
www.city.toronto.on.ca

Gage Park
Main St. East at Gage Ave.
Hamilton, ON
905–546–3780
e-mail: parks@city.hamilton.on.ca

Hancock Woodlands and Nurseries
2151 Camilla Road, Mississauga, ON
905–277–2961
www.hancockwoodlands.ca
e-mail: nursery@hancockwoodlands.ca

Jackson Park–Queen Elizabeth II Gardens
Tecumseh and Ouellette, Windsor, ON
519–253–2300

Lorne Park
Colbourne St. and Gilkenson Road
Brantford, ON
519–751–9900 (Brantford Tourism)
519–756–1500 (Brantford Parks and Recreation Dept.)

Mississauga Garden Park
N of Burnhamthorpe Road and W of Hwy. 403, Mississauga, ON
905–896–5371
www.city.mississauga.on.ca/rec&parks/html/parks/parks_home.htm

Niagara Parks Botanical Gardens
2565 Niagara Parkway, Niagara Falls, ON
905–356–8554 or
1–877–NIA–PARK
www.niagaraparks.com
e-mail: npinfo@niagaraparks.com

Queen Elizabeth Gardens in Chrysler Park
Upper Canada Village Heritage Park including the Memorial Garden and Pioneer Garden
13740 Country Road 2
RR1, Morrisburg, ON
800–437–2233

Royal Botanical Gardens
680 Plains Road West, Burlington, ON
905–527–1158
www.rbg.ca
e-mail: grow@rbg.ca

Stokes Seed Flower Trial Gardens
Adjacent to Lake Ontario on Lakeshore Road between 7th St. and 5th St.
St. Catharines, ON
800–396–9238
www.stokeseeds.com
e-mail: stokes@stokeseeds.com

University of Waterloo Gardens
200 University Ave. W, Waterloo, ON
519–888–4567
www.adm.uwaterloo.ca/infoipa/brochure/gardens.html

Walker Botanical Gardens
Rodman Hall Arts Centre
109 St. Paul Crescent, St. Catharines, ON
905–684–2925

ACKNOWLEDGEMENTS

I would especially like to thank my fellow garden writers, Don Williamson and Laura Peters, for their many contributions and discussions. As well, I would like to thank Peter Thompstone and the staff at the Niagara College Horticulture Department for their inspiration and continued assistance.

We are grateful to photographers Tamara Eder, Tim Matheson and Robert Ritchie, and to the many people who opened their gardens for us to photograph, both in Ontario and elsewhere. Thanks go to gardeners Tony and Milton Castelino, Ernst and Tamara Eder, Gerry Forestier, Trevor and Cherylynne Horbachewsky, Anita Jenkins, Lesley Knight, Bill Kozak, Heather Markham, Robert and Margery Ritchie, Heidi Clausen and Robert Ritchie, Alex Rosato and Jeff Ross. As well we'd like to thank the Agriculture Canada Central Experimental Farm, Casa Loma Gardens, Cullen Gardens, Edwards Gardens, the Niagara Parks Botanic Gardens, Rideau Hall and the Royal Botanical Gardens (Ontario); Montreal Botanic Gardens (Quebec); Devonian Botanic Garden, Greenland Garden Centre, La Boheme Restaurant, Laurel's Flower & Garden and the Muttart Conservatory (Alberta); Adamson's Heritage Nursery Ltd., Select Roses and VanDusen Botanical Garden (British Columbia); Chicago Botanic Gardens and Morton Arboretum (Illinois); Barbara and Douglas Bloom, Thea and Don Bloomquist and Cranbrook Gardens (Michigan); and the International Rose Test Garden (Oregon) for kindly allowing us to photograph their plants and gardens.

We would also like to thank Shane Kennedy, Nancy Foulds, editors Sandra Bit and Lee Craig, and designer and Master Gardener Heather Markham. The assistance of Jennifer Fafard and Carol Woo was also appreciated. Thanks also to Gerry Dotto for the cover design and to Ian Sheldon for the lovely corner flourishes that grace the pages. Others helped in various ways, close-cropping photos and providing stylistic solutions, and we thank them all.

❧

Cover page photos:
January–spruce bough; February–crabapple branches; March–forsythia blossoms; April–primroses and tulips; May–lilac flower; June–hosta; July–shrub rose 'The Fairy'; August–dahlias; September–viburnum (highbush cranberry); October–fall leaves; November–hoarfrost at sunset; December–poinsettias